Euroscepticism and the Future of Europe

Michael Kaeding • Johannes Pollak
Paul Schmidt
Editors

Euroscepticism and the Future of Europe

Views from the Capitals

Editors
Michael Kaeding
University of Duisburg-Essen
Duisburg, Germany

Johannes Pollak
Webster Vienna Private University
Vienna, Austria

Paul Schmidt
Austrian Society for European
Politics (ÖGfE)
Vienna, Austria

The European Commission's support for the production of this publication does not constitute an endorsement of the contents, which reflect the views only of the authors, and the Commission cannot be held responsible for any use which may be made of the information contained therein.

ISBN 978-3-030-41271-5   ISBN 978-3-030-41272-2 (eBook)
https://doi.org/10.1007/978-3-030-41272-2

© The Editor(s) (if applicable) and The Author(s), under exclusive licence to Springer Nature Switzerland AG 2021
This work is subject to copyright. All rights are solely and exclusively licensed by the Publisher, whether the whole or part of the material is concerned, specifically the rights of translation, reprinting, reuse of illustrations, recitation, broadcasting, reproduction on microfilms or in any other physical way, and transmission or information storage and retrieval, electronic adaptation, computer software, or by similar or dissimilar methodology now known or hereafter developed.
The use of general descriptive names, registered names, trademarks, service marks, etc. in this publication does not imply, even in the absence of a specific statement, that such names are exempt from the relevant protective laws and regulations and therefore free for general use.
The publisher, the authors and the editors are safe to assume that the advice and information in this book are believed to be true and accurate at the date of publication. Neither the publisher nor the authors or the editors give a warranty, expressed or implied, with respect to the material contained herein or for any errors or omissions that may have been made. The publisher remains neutral with regard to jurisdictional claims in published maps and institutional affiliations.

Cover illustration: Zbitnev

This Palgrave Macmillan imprint is published by the registered company Springer Nature Switzerland AG.
The registered company address is: Gewerbestrasse 11, 6330 Cham, Switzerland

Foreword

In May 2019, over 200 million Europeans elected 751 Members of European Parliament. With more than 50 percent, the turnout was the highest it has ever been in the past 25 years and represents an increase of 8.3 percentage points from the previous election in 2014. To illustrate, more citizens were entitled to vote at the European elections than the United States has inhabitants as a whole.

In contrast to certain predictions made by political commentators and spectators, the election result gives a clear pro-European mandate for more European engagement, more European solutions and more cooperation on a European level. Citizens voted because they want to see Europe taking action on a range of crucial issues from climate, jobs and the economy, to migration, security and defense.

Today, more citizens approve of the European Union than in previous decades. This is a direct result of multiple advantages, which have often become a matter of course on the one hand, such as the ability to easily work or study in another EU country. Political developments such as Brexit have tested and ultimately strengthened citizens commitment to the European Union. With the Brexit process slowly ending, the imperative lessons to be learned from this is that politics must be centered on compromise and cooperation instead of unconditional enforcement of political opinion or will. However, at the same time the Union also faces more challenges.

When looking beyond the borders, it becomes evident that peace, freedom, democracy and prosperity cannot be taken for granted. Even in Europe, war is still a daily occurrence when looking to Eastern Ukraine. In some EU Member states, liberal, parliamentary democracy is questioned and fundamental rights such as the rule of law are trampled on. Thirty years after the end of the unjust regimes in Eastern Europe and the fall of the Iron Curtain and the Berlin Wall, many citizens are concerned that the rule of law and liberal democracy are endangered.

There is one major lesson from the fall of communism. Regimes, which do not respect the rule of law, human and fundamental rights, can never ensure trust, freedom and fairness in a society. A country that does not have an independent judiciary that suppresses civil society and media freedom, and denies its citizens a fair living environment will fail to establish a relationship of trust.

A changing world also leads to rising pressures from inside and outside the Union. On the one hand, nationalists and populists seek to weaken or partially destroy the EU. On the other, world leaders such as President Trump challenge the global order by withdrawing from international treaties, expanding protectionism and questioning multilateralism. To withstand these developments, we need to make Europe stronger, more capable and more efficient.

We have to deal with populist and nationalist forces through substantial debates and practice oriented approaches in order to expose their dangerous ignorance.

They claim that taking back power from Brussels to the capitals through a Europe of Nations will subsequently solve all issues. Equally, they assert that Europe can be sustained with a halved or even abolished European Parliament. However, the terrifying reality behind these claims is a weakened Europe of uncoordinated small-scale states. More isolation, more nationalism, more demarcation and less cooperation and cohesion at European level. This would lead to economic decline and in particular the decline of the middle class, as well as the global insignificance of Europe. Europe is too valuable to be torn apart by populist and nationalist forces. On the contrary, we must work together to strengthen the Union and intensify cooperation. Together we must tackle issues like the fight against tax havens and money laundering, security policy, climate and environmental protection, investments, research and development as well as the competitiveness of small and medium-sized enterprises.

Thankfully, the tactics of populists, who play on feelings of insecurity, fear and blame, did not succeed at a European level during the 2019 elections. The majority of citizens throughout Europe realized that falling into populist traps would be contrary to the reality of what they were really voting for. To fulfil the expectations and deliver on the promises made, we have to develop the democratic decision-making mechanisms further. Only then, we will be able to improve efficiency, build our capacity to find solutions and take action on the issues most important to citizens.

This means that we must abolish the practice of unanimous voting in the Council with regard to certain decisions taken by Member States. This practice leads to unnecessary blockades, blackmail and the total incapacity of the EU to act even when action is urgently needed. We fare much better wherever the co-decision procedure applies, and the European Parliament and the Council are on equal footing in terms of deciding on EU legislation. There is a stark difference between policy areas where co-decision applies and those where the EU is paralysed by unanimous decisions to be taken by all Member States.

This means that instead of the unanimity of Member States, there must be majority decisions in all policy areas. A simple majority in the European Parliament and a "double majority" of the Member States. Meaning a majority of Member States representing the majority of the European population. This would be more democratic, more transparent and more efficient.

The idea of Europe will only have a bright future if the EU-citizens are part of it. Today, hundreds of millions of citizens feel at home across national borders. We live in the largest shared economic area in the world driven by the freedom of movement, the free movement of goods, services and capital. Let us allow our citizens to be a stronger part of the political process on the European level.

The European Parliament is a reflection of European society. Trust, fairness, freedom, prosperity and cooperation mutually exclude populism and nationalism and can therefore not coexist within the same train of political thought an argumentation. That is why we need a Conference on the future of Europe. We need a strong partnership with the EU citizen's apart from party politics. Let us put the future of Europe and the role of the European Union in the world above party lines. The future needs dialogue, European awareness and joint action.

European Parliament, Brussels, Belgium   Othmar Karas

WHY THIS BOOK?

Europeans no longer tacitly approve of European integration because of its positive effects on welfare and peace in a habitual manner. From the beginning political elites, citizens, media as well as civil society have criticised the European Union (EU), albeit to a different extent. Notably, political parties that are sceptical of the European integration process have become increasingly important over the past years across Europe—at a national and European level.

Europe has seen the rise, but also fall of Eurosceptic parties with nationalistic tendencies gaining further ground, fraying party systems with new parties and movements emerging and disappearing. On the one hand several Eurosceptic parties have taken up national executive responsibilities, have influenced the thinking of mainstream parties, swayed the public discourse with nationalistic, xenophobic, and anti-European rhetoric, and have further increased their number of parliamentarians in national and European parliamentary elections. Across Europe Eurosceptic parties are in government, support governments and successfully compete in parliamentary elections. On the other hand, some Eurosceptic parties never got into government, split up, left governments before the end of the legislative term or lost elections.

This book is an attempt to map and analyse the nature and impact of Euroscepticism in the different European party systems and take note of new nationalistic tendencies. The reason for this particular focus is that political parties are key gatekeepers in the process of political representation. They play a pivotal role in mobilizing societies and in setting the political agenda. In the end, they not only shape politics at a national level, but determine the way Europe plays out as a political issue and thus, define the very future of European integration.

We have asked authors from the 27 EU Member States as well as from the United Kingdom, Iceland, Liechtenstein, Norway, Switzerland, Turkey, Albania, Kosovo, Serbia, North Macedonia, Montenegro, Bosnia and Herzegovina and Ukraine to assess in short, concise op-eds the following questions: What influence do Eurosceptic parties have and how has it developed over the past years? Did the success of Eurosceptic parties in your country change the government's EU policy stance? If yes, in which areas? The authors take the reader on a journey through various political landscapes and sketch out recommendations on how each country should deal with Euroscepticism in light of the future of European integration. The contributors look at Europe through a decisively national lens precisely because Europe has more national capitals than it has in Brussels these days. Understanding what is happening in the European countries is a precondition to understand the dynamics of European integration.

THE 40 SHADES OF EUROSCEPTICISM ACROSS EUROPE

The manifold contributions reflect the diversity of Europe. Most of the countries display some form of Euroscepticism, notably the following aspects are apparent:

1. Euroscepticism is a longstanding phenomenon. In some countries, such as Austria, Belgium and Sweden Euroscepticism dates back to the early 1980s. While French Euroscepticism goes back to the 1992 referendum on the Maastricht Treaty, the entire political spectrum in Czechia has shifted towards a generalized Euroscepticism over the first 15 years of EU-membership.
2. Euroscepticism is still a recent phenomenon in newer EU member states. Today, Euroscepticism in Czechia is nigh omnipresent– in political debates, in the media and in the broader public sphere. Paradoxically, there are not many Czech parties that would call themselves Eurosceptic and those who would call for a Czexit are even fewer. Yet those who once simply preferred intergovernmental cooperation over federalization are now more or less openly nationalistic. In Croatia, the government's current political volatility is closely linked to a number of emerging new Eurosceptic parties and directly related to the financial and sovereign debt crisis

(mid-2000s) and the migration challenge (mid-2010s). Lately, many Estonians have become tired of being the EU's "poster child". They are afraid of imminent socio-economic changes, most prominently of immigration and migration. Consequently, a previously marginal anti-European populist party, the Conservative People's Party of Estonia (EKRE), started gaining popularity. EKRE has provided a forum to express this frustration in recent national and European elections.

3. Euroscepticism represents a self-standing cleavage cutting through the left-right divide. For the first time in France, for example, the 2017 Presidential elections were dominated by the European cleavage, dramatically framed by Macron as the confrontation between progressives and nationalists, open and closed society and liberal vs. illiberal democracy.
4. Euroscepticism is running out of steam in other countries. Polling suggests that it is losing ground in Denmark, for example, as the consequences of the UK's vote for Brexit becomes clearer. Pro-European politics have clearly taken the centre stage in the Netherlands and in Cyprus where Euroscepticism is decreasing too.
5. Euroscepticism is often playing with public sentiments and perceptions. As Eurosceptic parties quickly adapt to changes in public opinion a few remarkable exceptions, however, are worth mentioning: the pro-European positions taken by the vast majority of Greek parliamentary parties may misrepresent public opinion, which rather displays pessimism and diminished confidence in the EU. Eurobarometer surveys show that satisfaction with the EU is lowest in Greece. Greeks registered the 4th lowest score on the question of whether their country has overall benefited from being an EU member, the 2nd lowest on the question "my voice counts in the EU", and the 2nd highest percentage of wishing to express disagreement over national politics as the main reason for voting in the recent European Parliament elections. Poland is another example where a right-wing Eurosceptic coalition in power led by Law and Justice (PiS) coexists with one of the most pro-European societies in the European Union. According to recent opinion polls (COBOS 2019), 91 percent of Polish society declares to be positive about EU membership and only 5 percent think that Poland shouldn't be part of the EU.

6. Euroscepticism is (still) not prevalent in all European countries. In fact, four countries hardly display any form of Euroscepticism. Next to Ireland and Lithuania, Latvia has no Eurosceptic political party represented in the national parliament or municipalities. In the May 2019 European Parliament elections, none of the 13 political parties supported leaving the EU. At the same time, recent years have seen the emergence of EU intergovernmentalist positions in opposition to Latvia's traditional EU-federalist position. In addition, the Maltese party system is overwhelmingly Euro-enthusiastic showing some of the highest approval ratings for the EU. While Euroscepticism has been side-lined, nationalistic themes, however, have been gaining ground with the 2019 European elections in Malta, experiencing one of the most negative campaigns in Europe and that focused primarily on patriotism.
7. Euroscepticism occurs on the left and the right side of the political spectrum. With the exception of Austria, Cyprus, Denmark, Estonia, Hungary, Poland and Slovakia, most European countries have experienced right and left-wing Euroscepticism in parallel, while the left focuses their discourse largely on a rejection of the so-called "ultraliberal" Europe. In the 2019 European elections in France, for example, Eurosceptic parties scored up to 36 percent of the vote. Jean-Luc Mélenchon's France Unbowed (LFI) on the far left and Marine Le Pen's National Rally (RN, formerly National Front) on the far right, accounted together for 83 percent of these votes. In Croatia, compared with the results of 2016 national elections the Eurosceptic candidates increased their support during the 2019 European elections by a staggering 18 percent, scoring together more than 35 percent of the combined votes obtained by the Eurosceptic far-right (21.9 percent) and far-left (13.4 percent).
8. The number of Eurosceptic parties in national parliaments varies considerably. In the Netherlands, for example, five out of 13 parties in the Tweede Kamer share a (different) Eurosceptic agenda: the Forum for Democracy' (FvD) and the 'Freedom Party' (PVV), take the staunchest Eurosceptic positions, with the PVV advocating a 'Nexit' and the FvD calling for a membership referendum. The PvdD, SGP and SP propose less ambitious forms of EU cooperation, with the SP arguing to leave the eurozone, the PvdD arguing for a common currency among the Northern-European

countries and the SGP demanding a judicial mechanism making it possible to leave the eurozone and stay part of the EU.
9. Euroscepticism takes many forms. While some EU-countries (Lithuania and Czechia) have seen the most critical positions on the EU being expressed not by political parties but by political movements, Euroscepticism ranges from a few xenophobic parties, such as for example the Polish KONFEDERACJA or the Spanish VOX, to those demanding an exit strategy, such as the Slovak L'SNS or the Dutch PVV, to other hard and soft forms of Euroscepticism proclaiming more and more to "change Europe from within".
10. Euroscepticism in non-EU countries varies significantly too. Talking about Eurosceptic parties in Switzerland and Liechtenstein, for example, requires a serious recalibration of the concept. In comparison with EU Member States, all Swiss and Liechtenstein parties adhere to a hard version of Euroscepticism with no party currently advocating fast and full EU membership. Consequently, all political parties in Liechtenstein and Switzerland are Eurosceptic—some, however, more than others. The Swiss People's Party SVP and the Liechtenstein DpL are prototypes of the right-wing, nationalist and populist party that have thrived in many of the EU countries. In addition, the vast majority of Icelandic citizens support Iceland's membership in the European Economic Area (EEA) and Schengen, and there is a cross party consensus on membership in the European Free Trade Association (EFTA). However, the political party system is increasingly polarized around European integration. New Eurosceptic and pro-European parties have emerged, which campaign to limit Iceland's participation in the EEA and Schengen or join the EU. In the countries of the Western Balkans EU integration is considered a process to benefit the whole society, representing freedom and equality for all, and a chance to belong to a large family sharing progressive values. The European perspective has been a powerful engine for change in all six countries over the last two decades. It has become a key motivating factor behind the country's economic and political reforms. In other countries, populism is intertwined with anti-EU sentiments, but for the Western Balkan, the EU has been for a long time the popular choice. Although at this moment

EU-enlargement fatigue poses real risk of reversing some of the achievements of the accession process.
11. Euroscepticism is in constant flux. In Hungary, for example, there have been substantial shifts on the right wing of the political spectrum. JOBBIK, originally an anti-EU party has started to move towards the centre and has recognized the value added of EU membership, even if criticizing „Brussels interference into domestic issues" in specific policy areas. At the same time, the governing FIDESZ made a turn to the extreme right, mixing Euroscepticism with evident anti-EU attitude and open nationalistic rhetoric. Also, the German AfD (Alternative für Deutschland) has evolved from a Eurosceptic single-issue anti-Euro party in 2008, breaking with Germany's long-standing permissive consensus on European integration, to a hard version of Euroscepticism and nowadays leading the opposition party in the German Bundestag. In Greece, a new ultra-right nationalist-populist party, Greek Solution, which owes its existence to the nationalist sentiment unleashed in Greek Macedonia against the recognition of the neighbouring Republic of North Macedonia, has succeeded the far-right Golden Dawn, which failed to enter Parliament, as well as the nationalist-populist Independent Greeks (ANEL), a former coalition partner of SYRIZA in government, which scored below the 3 percent threshold.

Impact of Eurosceptic Parties

From senior to junior coalition partner in national government to opposition leader and notorious backbenchers, the degrees of impact of Eurosceptic parties vary considerably. Debates across Europe continue whether to embrace or marginalize Eurosceptic parties. For example, in Sweden the political elite wonders whether to include the Sweden Democrats on specific issues without running the risk of being influenced by their lack of respect for certain values. The Left Party, the Social Democrats, the Green Party, the Centre Party and the Liberals are strongly against it, whereas the Christian Democrats and the Moderates seem increasingly positive on the issue of integrating them. So far, no cooperation has yet been initiated at the national level—in contrast to Norway and Finland. In Bulgaria, forms of cooperation have led to an increasing number of Eurosceptic parties. Forming minority governments in 2009 and 2014, the Bulgarian GERB relied on the tacit support of Attack. This initiated the creeping legitimization of nationalism and Euroscepticism in mainstream politics, with increasing numbers of Eurosceptic parties such as the Patriotic Front—(NFSB and IMRO), entering the parliament in 2014 and a new populist party—WILL, in 2017.

In Austria, the Austrian Freedom Party (FPÖ), part of the political landscape for more than 60 years, has been a junior coalition partner three times since the year 2000 with varying impact. Nowadays, it is the only relevant political force pursuing an explicit Eurosceptic agenda but has massively lost support in the latest elections. As junior coalition partner the FPÖ refrained from radical anti-Euro and anti-EU rhetoric in public, in particular during Austria's EU Council Presidency. Yet, the party questioned the legal basis of the infringement procedures against Hungary and promoted the rejection of the UN global migration pact.

In the opposition, the impact of Eurosceptic positions can still be significant. The Danish DPP for instance may have lost votes in recent national and European elections, but it has heavily influenced both the Danish Liberals and Social Democrats, the two largest Danish governing parties, over the past two decades. The Liberals, thus, lost the general election after it was outfoxed by the Social Democrats on taking its immigration policy further to the right and toning down its pro-EU rhetoric. The 'taking in' of the positions of the far right has probably gone further in Denmark than anywhere else in Europe. In Denmark's public discourse it is considered almost absurd to even question the political legitimacy of the far right today.

Also, the reluctance of the French Socialist Prime Minister Manuel Valls (2014–2017) to welcome refugees can be understood as a consequence of the continuous rise of Marine Le Pen and the radical RN.

Albeit strong tensions and fractions between the political parties in Spain, there has traditionally been a national consensus regarding the value of European integration and the benefits of EU membership. With some of the new parties performing rather well, consensus is becoming more and more fragile. Spain has ceased being a stronghold of pro-European political parties. It is not immune anymore against the rise of Euroscepticism with the very right-wing party Vox having gained close to 15 percent of the vote share in the latest national parliamentary elections making it the third biggest party in the Spanish parliament. The left-wing party Podemos is likely to enter a government coalition and the proponents of independence in Catalonia will use their regional political weight to gain further autonomy.

The Luxembourgish Eurosceptic ADR's vocal claim that the Luxembourgish language should be reassessed at European level also left its footprint. In light of the recognition of other small European languages such as Irish and Maltese as official EU languages, the Luxembourgish government launched an action plan to promote Luxembourgish as a vehicle of communication (besides the country's two other official languages, French and German) and to make Luxembourgish one of the official languages of the European Union.

In Switzerland the SVP's impact on Switzerland's EU policy is disproportionate to its vote share. Not only has it taken the option of EU membership off the political agenda. The SVP's capacity to campaign successfully on Swiss values such as neutrality, sovereignty and direct democracy against the alleged democratic deficits, foreign judges and power grabs of the EU constrains the institutional deepening of bilateralism. Moreover, the SVP's regular launch of popular votes against the perceived costs of integration—such as immigration or financial contributions to the EU's cohesion policy—polarizes Swiss politics and keeps EU-Swiss relations in a stranglehold.

Clearly, party-based Euroscepticism is part of the political *Landschaft* of most Member States and beyond, and government responses to it throughout Europe is as diverse as civil societies. Eurosceptic parties are by no means in retreat, they are "here to stay" (Treib, 2019). This volume of argumentative, op-ed style short chapters covering 40 European countries highlights this diversity. Eurosceptic parties might not always be strong enough to enter governments or remain in government for a full period, but their views increasingly enter mainstream politics.

How Should We Address Party Political Euroscepticism in Light of the Future of European Integration?

There is a clear need for focusing on the main social drivers of Euroscepticism: unemployment, socioeconomic vulnerability, climate change and widespread insecurities, morphing into not just anti-EU sentiment but anti-immigrant and xenophobic stances. Without a credible re-invention of Europe's priorities addressing those issues such negative stances will persist and represent an ever-bigger challenge for the European integration project and its liberal values. Governments across the continent have the obligation to define objectives that reach beyond the electoral cycle. Europe has served them all incredibly well, what it needs now is a spelling out of a captivating vision of the future. It matters less if this vision is federalist or intergovernmentalist. What matters is that it recognises the value of cooperation, the advantage of many years of trust building amongst neighbours bound together by not only geography but also heritage and values. There is a need for a genuine public debate on the pros and cons of further European integration which has been less pronounced in the last decade. This would foster awareness of the degree of integration that has already reached and the benefits it harbours. There is a need to include the demands and visions of the younger generation to a much higher degree. For those ideas to be productive, they need to be built on a better understanding of Europe's past.

It is essential to continue strengthening bilateral relations with non-EU countries and to maintain a clear EU perspective. In the Western Balkans, in particular, the EU can extract further benefits from deepening this alliance by keeping the enlargement perspective open and by pushing through a reform agenda that makes the region more attractive for EU investors. Anything short of a strong EU-presence will jeopardise the reforms, the countries' democratic future, and create a vacuum that will be exploited by anti-reformist and anti-EU forces. In Turkey, despite the political situation, the EU should engage with those parts of Turkish civil society, which still strive for democratic governance.

After all this volume talks to an audience beyond the normal academic niche interested in European politics. It is a guidebook through a tremendously dynamic, interesting and challenging political landscape. And as a guidebook it favours the lexical purpose as much as the comprehensive comparative reading. Students and teachers may find a myriad of questions to explore deeper in seminar papers and theses. Practitioners will benefit from the overview it presents. And for all of us it shows the breath-taking diversity that unites this continent.

We would like to thank Pol VILA SARRIÁ, project officer at TEPSA, for the editorial processing and his tireless efforts to make this project happen.

Michael Kaeding
Johannes Pollak
Paul Schmidt

Contents

Albania: Will the EU's Ambiguity Lead to Euroscepticism?   1
Leonie Vrugtman

Austria: Taking a Walk on the Wild Side   5
Paul Schmidt

Belgium: Breaking the Consensus? Eurosceptic Parties   9
Wouter Wolfs and Steven Van Hecke

Bosnia and Herzegovina: Ethnopolitics and Hopeful
Euroscepticism—No Light at the End of the European Tunnel?   13
Vedran Džihić

Bulgaria: Creeping EU-Scepticism—The Tacit Consent that
Fuels Populism   17
Hristo Panchugov and Ivan Nachev

Croatia: The Government Should Take Citizens Seriously   21
Hrvoje Butković

Cyprus: A Pro-European Attitude, but Scepticism Still Holds
Strong   25
Giorgos Kentas

Czechia: Who Is the Most Eurosceptic of Them All? The
Eurosceptic Race to the Bottom 29
Zdeněk Sychra and Petr Kratochvíl

Denmark: Ambivalence Towards the EU—From Foot-
Dragging to Pacesetters? 35
Maja Kluger Dionigi and Marlene Wind

Estonia: Challenges with the Popularity of Right-Wing
Radicalism 39
Viljar Veebel

Finland: A Meaningful EU Debate Is Needed to Regain
Ground from Populist Framing 43
Juha Jokela

France: When Euroscepticism Becomes the Main Credo of the
Opposition 47
Nonna Mayer and Olivier Rozenberg

Germany: Eurosceptics and the Illusion of an Alternative 51
Katrin Böttger and Funda Tekin

Greece: The Remarkable Defeat of Euroscepticism 55
George Pagoulatos

Hungary: Euroscepticism and Nationalism 59
András Inotai

Iceland: Hard-Line Eurosceptics Clash with Eurosceptics 65
Baldur Thorhallsson

Ireland: 'A Rising Tide Lifts All Boats'—A Unique Situation
on Countering Euroscepticism 69
Róisín Smith

Italy: Has Salvini Saved the Country from Himself? Not Yet   73
Eleonora Poli

Kosovo: Moonwalking Towards the European Union   77
Venera Hajrullahu

Latvia: Euroscepticism—Between Reason and Treason   81
Karlis Bukovskis and Andris Spruds

Liechtenstein: Euroscepticism Yes and No!   85
Christian Frommelt

Lithuania: Euroscepticism—Present on the Margins   89
Ramūnas Vilpišauskas

Luxembourg: Make Europe Work Better in the Greater Regions   93
Guido Lessing

Malta: Bucking the Trend—How Malta Turned its Back on Euroscepticism   97
Mark Harwood

Montenegro: A Great Bargain Between the European Union Optimism and Real Euroscepticism   101
Danijela Jaćimović and Sunčica Rogic

North Macedonia: The Name in Exchange for European Union Membership?   105
Irena Rajchinovska Pandeva

Norway: Outside, But ...   109
John Erik Fossum

Poland: Economic Enthusiasts, Value Adversaries   115
Zdzisław Mach and Natasza Styczyńska

Portugal: Something Old, Something New
and Everything Blue   119
Alice Cunha

Romania: Euroscepticism—Contamination of the Mainstream
Parties, Limited Support Among the Citizens   123
Bianca Toma and Alexandru Damian

Serbia: Our Greatest Fear—An Empty Country, Pawn in the
Hands of Great Powers on the "Periphery of the Periphery"   127
Marko Savković

Slovakia: Euroscepticism as a Changing Notion in Electoral
Campaigns   131
Oľga Gyárfášová and Lucia Mokrá

Slovenia: Extremes Are Attractive Only to the Media   135
Maja Bučar and Boštjan Udovič

Spain: The Risk of Too High Expectations on the EU's Role
as a Problem Solver   139
Ignacio Molina

Sweden: Battling for Values   145
Gunilla Herolf

Switzerland: A Vital Relationship in the Stranglehold of
Euroscepticism   149
Frank Schimmelfennig

The Netherlands: Playing with Fire? Dutch Political Parties
Between Reluctant and Pragmatic Pro-Europeanism   153
Maurits J. Meijers, Lars Stevenson, and Adriaan Schout

Turkey: A Vicious Cycle of Euroscepticism? 159
Senem Aydın-Düzgit and Özgehan Şenyuva

UK: Brexit—The Car That Keeps on Crashing 163
Brendan Donnelly

Ukraine: The Progress of (Euro) Populism in Postmodern Age 167
Yuriy Yakymenko and Viktor Zamiatin

Index 171

Notes on Contributors

Senem Aydın-Düzgit is Professor of International Relations at the Faculty of Arts and Social Sciences of Sabancı University and Academic Affairs Coordinator of the Istanbul Policy Center.
Founded in 2001, the Istanbul Policy Center (IPC) is a global policy research institution that specializes in key social and political issues ranging from democratization to climate change, transatlantic relations to conflict resolution and mediation. The IPC offers policymakers, academics, and young researchers a unique platform where sound academic research in social sciences shapes hands-on policy work.

Katrin Böttger is Director at the Institut für Europäische Politik, Berlin. She holds several honorary board memberships including the European Community Studies Association Germany, the European Movement Germany, TEPSA and the Centre international de formation européene, where she also teaches.
The Institute for European Politics (IEP) is a German non-profit organization dedicated to the study of European integration. IEP is a member of TEPSA.

Maja Bučar is a Professor at the Faculty of Social Sciences of the University of Ljubljana and the Head of the Centre of International Relations. Her main field of teaching and research is in international political economy, development studies, European Union development/research and development policies. She has been involved in a number of international and national projects, related to the above topics.

Centre of International Relations (CIR) conducts interdisciplinary research in the fields of international relations, international economics and international business, politics of international law, diplomacy, human rights, international organisations, and European integration. CIR is a long-standing and active member of TEPSA as well as several other international networks.

Karlis Bukovskis is Deputy Director of the Latvian Institute of International Affairs, and the author of numerous articles, and the scientific editor of several books. Bukovskis is an Assistant Professor at Riga Stradins University on global political economy, and the international financial system and the European Union.

The Latvian Institute of International Affairs (LIIA) is the oldest Latvian think tank that specializes in foreign and security policy analysis. LIIA is an independent research institute that conducts research, develops publications and organizes public lectures and conferences related to global affairs and Latvia's international role and policies. LIIA is a member of TEPSA.

Hrvoje Butković is Senior Research Associate at the Department for European Integration of the Institute for Development and International Relations (IRMO) in Zagreb, Croatia. He defended his PhD in 2010, at the Faculty of Political Science of the University of Zagreb. His primary research interests include the EU institutions, democracy in the EU and industrial relations in Europe.

The Institute for Development and International Relations (IRMO) is a public, non-profit, scientific research organization stationed in Zagreb, Croatia. Its main work is organized through four departments. IRMO provides strategic support to decision-makers and ensures the dissemination of its research results. IRMO is part of TEPSA.

Alice Cunha is Research Fellow at the Portuguese Institute of International Relations. She is the author of several publications and has a special research interest in European Integration and EU funding.

The Portuguese Institute of International Relations (IPRI) is a research unit of NOVA University, dedicated to advanced studies in Political Science, International Relations and European Integration. IPRI is a member of TEPSA.

Alexandru Damian is a Researcher at the Romanian Centre for European Policies. He is involved in projects related to foreign affairs, the Eastern

Partnership, the judiciary and anti-corruption. He is a graduate of Political Science and has an MA in European Union Studies from the Free University of Brussels.

The Romanian Centre for European Policies (CRPE) is one of the leading Romanian think-tanks specialized in EU affairs, with over 10 years of experience in implementing European and regional projects. The mission of the CRPE is to promote Romania as an influential leader in the development of EU agendas and policies. Another major objective is to advance the Europeanization processes in Romania and to promote European citizenship by providing expertise in various fields and by initiating or participating in public debates. CRPE is a member of TEPSA.

Brendan Donnelly is Director of the Federal Trust, a pro-European think tank in London. He is a former Member of the European Parliament (1994 to 1999). He was educated at Oxford and later worked in the Foreign Office, the European Parliament and the European Commission. He is the author of "On the Edge: Britain and Europe" (jointly with Hugh Dykes; 2012) and written numerous articles on the European Union (EU), Britain's place in the EU and federalism.

The Federal Trust is a think tank that studies the interactions between regional, national, European and global levels of government. Founded in 1945 on the initiative of Sir William Beveridge, it has long made a powerful contribution to the study of federalism and federal systems. The Federal Trust is a member of TEPSA.

Vedran Džihić is Senior Researcher at the Austrian Institute for International Affairs (OIIP), Co-Director of the Center for Advanced Studies, South East Europe, and Senior Lecturer at the Institute for Political Sciences, University of Vienna. He is a non-resident Fellow at the Center for Transatlantic Relations (SAIS), John Hopkins University, Washington D.C. Dzihic is the author of 4 monographs and editor/co-editor of 15 edited volumes/books. He is also the author of numerous book chapters and scholarly articles (in journals like Nationalities Papers, East European Politics and Society, Southeastern Europa, Journal of Southeast European and Black Sea Studies, JEMIE, Europe-Asia Studies, etc.).

The Austrian Institute for International Affairs (OIIP) is a Think Tank founded in 1979 and committed to fundamental research in the field of international politics. The OIIP is Austria's leading institute on international politics at the juncture between academic and policy-oriented research.

John Erik Fossum is Professor at ARENA Centre for European Studies, University of Oslo, Norway. He has worked and published widely on issues of identity, democracy and constitutionalism in the EU and Canada. He is project coordinator for the H2020-project EU3D—Differentiation, Dominance, Democracy (2019–2023). His most recent books are: Squaring the Circle on Brexit—Could the Norway Model Work? (2018), with Hans Petter Graver; Diversity and Contestations over Nationalism in Europe and Canada, (2018), co-edited with Riva Kastoryano and Birte Siim, and Towards a Segmented European Political Order, co-edited with Jozef Batora (2019).

ARENA is a multidisciplinary centre of basic research at the University of Oslo studying the evolving European political order.

Christian Frommelt is the Director of the Liechtenstein Institute in Bendern, Liechtenstein, since 2018. He has been a research fellow in Political Science at the Institute since 2010. He holds a PhD from the Swiss Federal Institute of Technology (ETH) in Zurich as well as a Master's degree from the University of Innsbruck. His research focuses on the European Economic Area (EEA) and on the integration policies of the European Free Trade Association (EFTA) Member states. Additionally, he has been Director for Brexit Studies at the Ministry of Foreign Affairs, Justice and Culture of Liechtenstein (2017–2018).

The Liechtenstein Institute was founded in 1986 as a research institute for scientific research in the fields of history, politics, law and economy relating to Liechtenstein. The Institute is organised as a non-profit association and is state-subsidized. The Institute is a full member of TEPSA.

Oľga Gyárfášová is Associate Professor and Senior Researcher at the Institute of European Studies and International Relations, Comenius University in Bratislava. She studied sociology and holds a PhD in comparative political science. In her research she focuses on electoral studies, political culture, analyses of populism and right-wing extremism. She is also a national coordinator of the European Election Studies (EES).

The Faculty of Social and Economic Sciences is an integral part of the Comenius University in Bratislava. Academics and researchers provide expertise in different fields of social sciences for national decision-makers as well as run research and popularisation projects in Slovakia and abroad.

The international environment at the faculty involves also foreign professors, international students and acquisition of European research projects. In the last decade the faculty is considered to be one of the best social science faculties in Slovakia. The Institute of European Studies is a member of TEPSA.

Venera Hajrullahu graduated from the Faculty of Philology at the University of Pristina. She also studied European Affairs at the European Institute of the University of Geneva and completed Executive Education on Strategic Management for Leaders of Non-Governmental Organizations at the Harvard Kennedy School. She is the Founder and Director of Change Experts Group and was the Executive Director of the Kosovar Civil Society Foundation and Chair of the Balkan Civil Society Development Network. Prior to that, she was Director of the European Integration Processes Office in the Office of the Prime Minister and then served as an Advisor on European Affairs to the Prime Minister of Kosovo. She was a Member of the Steering Committee of the Regional School of Public Administration (RESPA) and Member of the Council of the Independent Media Commission of Kosovo. She has chaired experts' groups and thematic tables for the Strategy of Public Administration Reform (PAR) and the Strategy for European Integration of Kosovo.

"Change Experts Group" is a network of top academics, practitioners, politicians and senior civil servants in Western Balkans and European Union (EU), specializing in democratic institution building, regional cooperation and EU integration

Mark Harwood is Director of the Institute for European Studies at the University of Malta. Having previously worked for the European Commission as well as the Maltese Government, his area of research is the impact of EU membership on Malta.

The Institute for European Studies was founded in 1991, and it is a teaching and research institute within the University of Malta. Offering a full range of degree programmes up to PhDs, the Institute has over 750 alumni. The Institute is a member of TEPSA.

Gunilla Herolf (PhD Stockholm University) is a Senior Associate Research Fellow at the Swedish Institute of International Affairs (SIIA/ UI) and Member of the Royal Swedish Academy of War Sciences (Vice

President 2010–2014), previously Senior Researcher at the Stockholm International Peace Research Institute (SIPRI).
SIIA/UI is an independent institute for research, analysis and information, founded in 1938.

András Inotai is Professor Emeritus, and former Director General of the Institute of World Economics (1991–2011). He taught in Peru (1972–1973), the College of Europe Bruges and Warsaw (1993–2017), Columbia University (2002) and in various other International Institutions (global economic issues, European integration, economic transition in Central and Eastern Europe). He is a Member of the Academic Council of the College of Europe, Scientific Board Member of the Bertelsmann Foundation and the author of several books and hundreds of professional articles mainly in English, German, Spanish and Hungarian. He holds various international and Hungarian awards.
The Institute for World Economics of the Hungarian Academy of Sciences (IWE) is an independent full-fledged research institute dedicated to the analysis of policy-oriented topics based on in-depth theoretical and methodological background. Its priority research areas include global economic developments, current and future challenges of the European Union including the evaluation of accession processes, international relations, the role of foreign direct investments and regional economic integration. IWE is a member of TEPSA.

Danijela Jaćimović is a Professor at the Faculty of Economics of the University of Montenegro. Her interests include International Economics and European Integration.
The University of Montenegro is the oldest higher education institution in Montenegro. The Faculty of Economics is one of the most important educational and research institutions in the country, with over 6000 students.

Juha Jokela is Director of the EU research programme at the Finnish Institute of International Affairs (FIIA). He is also a board member of TEPSA. His research interests include the political implications of Brexit, differentiated integration in the EU's external relations and Europeanisation of foreign policy.
FIIA is a research institute whose mission is to produce high-quality, topical information on international relations and the EU. FIIA is part of TEPSA.

Michael Kaeding is Jean Monnet Professor for European Integration and European Union Politics at the Institute of Political Science of the University of Duisburg-Essen. He is visiting fellow of the European Institute of Public Administration in Maastricht and member of the flying faculties of the College of Europe, Bruges, and the Turkish-German University in Istanbul. He is a Fulbright alumnus and received a one-semester Carl Schurz Professorship during the academic year 2019–2020 at the University of Madison-Wisconsin. His research covers books and articles on non-voters at European Parliament elections; the micromanagement of European institutions; implementation of EU-legislation, norms and values across Europe; and forms of classic and alternative EU decision-making. Between 2016–2019 he was the chairman of the Trans European Policy Studies Association.

The Institute of Political Science at the University Duisburg-Essen is the largest educational and research institution for political science in the federal state of North Rhine-Westphalia (NRW) and enjoys high standing within the German political science community.

Giorgos Kentas is Associate Professor in International Politics and Governance at the Department of Politics and Governance at the University of Nicosia. He is Director of a Master Program in Public Administration. His research focuses on strategic management, politics and governance at the national and European level. He follows EU developments and studies their implications for Member States and world politics. Recently he has published a paper on Brexit and its implications for Cyprus and a paper on strategic planning in the public sector of Cyprus.

The University of Nicosia is the largest private university in Cyprus. It offers more than 100 conventional and distance learning online programs at the Bachelor, Master and Doctorate level. It hosts more than 11,500 students from all over the world and it is a member of TEPSA.

Maja Kluger Dionigi is Senior Researcher at Think Tank Europa and External Lecturer at the University of Copenhagen. She holds a PhD in Government from the London School of Economics and Political Science (LSE). Her research focuses on legislative politics in the European Union, lobbying, transparency and accountability in European Union decision-making.

Think Tank Europa is an independent think tank that focuses on European issues and is dedicated to finding constructive and forward-looking answers to Denmark's role in the European Union.

Petr Kratochvíl is a Senior Researcher of the Institute of International Relations Prague and a Member of the TEPSA Board. He is the author of dozens of monographs, book chapters and journal articles. His research interests cover theories of international relations, European studies, and the religion-politics nexus.

The Institute of International Relations Prague (IIR) is an independent public research institution which has been conducting scholarly research in the area of international relations since 1957. As an institution originally founded by the Ministry of Foreign Affairs of the Czech Republic, the IIR also provides policy analysis and recommendations. It tries to form a link between the academic world, the public and international political practice. The IIR is a member of TEPSA.

Guido Lessing is Research Assistant at the Centre for Contemporary and Digital History (C^2DH) at the University of Luxembourg. His main field of interest is European integration and Public History.

The Luxembourg Centre for Contemporary and Digital History (C^2DH) is the University of Luxembourg's third interdisciplinary research centre, focusing on high-quality research, analysis and public dissemination in the field of contemporary Luxembourgish and European history. It promotes an interdisciplinary approach with a particular focus on new digital methods and tools for historical research and teaching.

Zdzisław Mach is Professor of sociology, social anthropology and European Studies at the Jagiellonian University in Krakow, Poland. He is the founder of the Institute for European Studies at the Jagiellonian University, UNESCO Chair for Education about the Holocaust and one of the main authors of the European Studies curriculum in Poland. His research interests cover issues such as nationalism, minorities and ethnicity, the development of European citizenship, migration, cultural construction of identities, collective memory and cultural heritage as well as the development of the idea of Europe. Professor Mach has been leading teams of researchers in the Polish National Science Centre and EU supported projects, including 6th Framework Programme and Horizon 2020.

The Institute for European Studies is a part of the Faculty of International and Political Studies at Jagiellonian University—the oldest and the leading university in Poland. The Institute is famous for its interdisciplinary approach that combines the perspectives of anthropology, economy, cultural studies, political sciences, history, law, and sociology.

Nonna Mayer is CNRS (National Centre for Scientific Research) Research Professor Emerita in Political Science at the Centre for European Studies and Comparatives Politics of Sciences Po. Her fields of expertise are electoral sociology, right-wing extremism, racism and antisemitism. She has written several books and articles on the Populist Radical Right in Europe and particularly the French National Rally.

Sciences Po is the leading French research university in Political Science, International Relations and Sociology. The Centre d'Etudes Européennes is a research centre which has been founded at Sciences Po in 2005. With an objective to fulfil three main missions: develop research on European questions at Sciences Po; to facilitate Sciences Po's insertion in European research networks; and to foster the European debate on the future of Europe. The Institute is a member of TEPSA.

Maurits J. Meijers is Assistant Professor of Comparative Politics at the Department of Political Science at the Institute for Management Research, Radboud University, Nijmegen, the Netherlands.

Radboud University is a public university with a strong focus on research located in Nijmegen, the Netherlands.

Lucia Mokrá is Associate Professor of International and European law at Comenius University in Bratislava, Faculty of Social and Economic Sciences. She is also a visiting teacher at other universities across Europe and chairperson of TEPSA's board. Her research includes human rights, external relations, institutional setting and enforcement in international and European law.

The Faculty of Social and Economic Sciences is an integral part of the Comenius University in Bratislava. Academics and researchers provide expertise in different fields of social sciences for national decision-makers as well as run research and popularisation projects in Slovakia and abroad. The international environment at the faculty involves also foreign professors, international students and acquisition of European research projects. In the last decade the faculty is considered to be one of the best social science faculties in Slovakia. The Institute of European Studies is a member of TEPSA.

Ignacio Molina is Senior Analyst at the Elcano Royal Institute and a Lecturer at the Department of Politics and International Relations at the Universidad Autónoma de Madrid. He holds a Ph.D. in Political Science from the same university. He is the author of many publications, including books, chapters in comparative volumes, articles in academic journals and policy papers. He has served as an external expert or consultant to several institutions. His areas of interest and expertise include the foreign and EU policy of Spain, and Europeanisation of Spain's politics and government.

The Elcano Royal Institute is a Spanish think tank for international studies. It is based in Madrid and was created in 2001 as a private foundation. The goal is to foster the creation and exchange of ideas in a plural and independent environment, with a stable and multidisciplinary team of analysts and a wide-ranging network of associated experts. The Elcano Institute takes its name from the Basque navigator who completed the first world circumnavigation five centuries ago.

Ivan Nachev is a Bulgarian political scientist, and an expert on political integration of the European Union. His interests are in the fields of political theory and practice, European values, European integration theories, strategies and political practices. He is a member of the Bulgarian Association for Political Sciences, the Institute for Public Policies and Partnership, the European Community Studies Association (ECSA) and Team Europe at the European Commission.

He has been the Head of Political Science Department at New Bulgarian University (NBU) in Sofia since 2012. He is Assistant Professor of European Integration and Political Theory at NBU since 1997. He has been secretary in a political section of the project "Europe 2000" at the Centre for the Study of Democracy, between 1995 and 1997, and a director of the *Bulgarian Examiner* magazine before that.

George Pagoulatos is Professor of European Politics and Economy at Athens University of Economics & Business, and Director General of ELIAMEP.

The Hellenic Foundation for European and Foreign Policy (ELIAMEP) is an independent, non-governmental, non-profit think tank established in Athens, Greece, in 1988. Its mission is to conduct policy-oriented research and provide policymakers, academics and the public at large with authoritative information and substantiated policy recommendations, to contribute to the development of evidence-based responses to major European and foreign policy challenges.

Hristo Panchugov is Assistant Professor at the Department of Political Science of the New Bulgarian University. He is Executive Director of the Democratic Institute Foundation. He graduated from the Central European University (Hungary).

The New Bulgarian University was established in 1991 with a resolution of the Bulgarian Parliament. The mission of the New Bulgarian University is to be an autonomous liberal education institution dedicated to the advancement of university education by offering accessible and affordable opportunities for interdisciplinary and specialized education and research of high quality.

Eleonora Poli is a Research Fellow at the Istituto Affari Internazionali (IAI), where she is working on the links between populism and economic governance in the EU and Western Balkans. Eleonora holds a PhD in International Political Economy from City University London. She has worked as a consultant for a number of prominent international organisations and public institutions and she is the author of "Antitrust Institutions and Policies in the Globalising Economy" (Palgrave Macmillan 2016) as well as several book chapters, opinion pieces, articles and analysis on the EU democratic trends and economic policies.

IAI is a private, independent non-profit think tank, founded in 1965 on the initiative of Altiero Spinelli, to promote awareness of international politics and contribute to the advancement of European integration and multilateral cooperation. IAI is a member of TEPSA.

Johannes Pollak is Professor of International Relations and rector of Webster Vienna Private University. Prior to this position, he headed the Department for Political Science at the Institute for Advanced Studies in Vienna. In summer 2019, he was elected chairperson of the Board of the Institute of European Politics in Berlin. Former positions include a Leverhulme Fellowship at the University of Reading, a Senior Visiting Fellowship at the LSE, and Jean Monnet Fellowship at the EUI in Florence. His research attempts to bridge political theory and European integration, and European energy policy. His latest book, with the University of Chicago Press deals with the theoretical challenges to political representation.

Webster University is an American university founded in 1915. The Vienna Campus, Webster Vienna Private University, opened in 1981 and is accredited both in the USA and in Austria.

Irena Rajchinovska Pandeva is an Associate Professor in political science at the Iustinianus Primus Law Faculty at the Ss. Cyril and Methodius University in Skopje. She is also vice-dean for science and international cooperation of the Faculty and Faculty Erasmus Coordinator and TEPSA's board member.

The Iustinianus Primus Law Faculty –Skopje is the oldest institution of higher education in the country offering legal studies program and is part of the Ss. Cyril and Methodius University in Skopje and the first public University in North Macedonia. The Faculty houses five different types of studies: legal, political science (in English and Macedonian language), journalism and public relations, in both undergraduate and postgraduate level. Its institutes and research units conduct research projects in law, political science, media and communications and European Union affairs. The Faculty is a member of TEPSA.

Sunčica Rogic is a PhD candidate and Teaching Assistant at the Faculty of Economics of the University of Montenegro.

The University of Montenegro is the oldest higher education institution in Montenegro. The Faculty of Economics is one of the most important educational and research institutions in the country, with over 6000 students.

Olivier Rozenberg is Associate Professor in Political Science at the Centre for European Studies and Comparatives Politics of Sciences Po. He specialises in the study of European integration and legislature. He has edited several books on those issues and the role of national parliaments in the European integration.

Sciences Po is the leading French research university in Political Science, International Relations and Sociology. The Centre d'Etudes Européennes is a research centre which has been founded at Sciences Po in 2005. With an objective to fulfil three main missions: develop research on European questions at Sciences Po; to facilitate Sciences Po's insertion in European research networks; and to foster the European debate on the future of Europe. The Institute is a member of TEPSA.

Marko Savković is Program Director at the Belgrade Fund for Political Excellence (BFPE). Previously, Marko worked for seven years as a researcher in the Belgrade Centre for Security Policy (BCSP), specialising in the fields of defence reform, civil-military relations and Euro-Atlantic integration. Marko holds a PhD from the Belgrade Faculty of Political Science. His work and thoughts have been published extensively in academic journals as well as various magazines and portals. He regularly writes for Novi magazin weekly and Danas daily newspapers. Marko is a member of the working groups dedicated to chapter 31 (Foreign, Security and Defence Policy) and 35 (Other issues: Kosovo) of Serbia's European integration process, within the National Convention on the EU.

The Belgrade Fund for Political Excellence (BFPE) is a non-governmental, non-partisan and non-profit organization founded in Serbia in 2003. For the last decade, the BFPE has been providing education and training to Serbian political and civil society leaders active in various sectors and engaged in reform processes.

Frank Schimmelfennig is Professor of European Politics at the Center for Comparative and International Studies, ETH Zurich, Switzerland. He is a Fellow of the Robert Schuman Center for Advanced Studies at the European University Institute, Florence, and heads the Academic Advisory Board of the Institut für Europäische Politik, Berlin. He is also a member of the TEPSA board. Frank Schimmelfennig works on European integration theory with a current focus on differentiated integration and the crisis of European integration. His most recent book is 'Ever Looser Union? Differentiated European Integration' (Oxford University Press 2020, with Thomas Winzen).

The Center for Comparative and International Studies is a joint research centre for political scientists at the ETH Zurich and the University of Zurich and offers a joint Master's program (MACIS).

Paul Schmidt is the Secretary General of the Austrian Society for European Politics, which promotes and supports analysis and communication on European affairs. Prior to that he has worked at the Oesterreichische Nationalbank, both in Vienna and at their Representative Office in Brussels at the Permanent Representation of Austria to the European Union. Paul currently dedicates his time to the analysis and discussion of topical issues regarding European integration, with a special focus on the development of

EU public opinion. His comments and op-eds are regularly published in Austrian as well as international media.
The Austrian Society for European Politics (Österreichische Gesellschaft für Europapolitik) was founded in 1991 and aims to promote and support communication and analysis of European affairs in Austria. With its headquarters in Vienna, the Society is a non-governmental and non-partisan platform mainly constituted by the Austrian Social Partners and the Oesterreichische Nationalbank. The Society is a member of TEPSA.

Adriaan Schout is Coordinator of EU Affairs and Senior Research Fellow at the Netherlands Institute of International Relations "Clingendael, The Hague, The Netherlands.
The Netherlands Institute of International Relations ('Clingendael') is a think tank and diplomatic training institute situated in The Hague. The Clingendael European Studies Programme (CESP) consists of ten researchers and trainers who work closely together with the other Clingendael Programmes. Its main objective is to contextualise current European Union developments in the longer-term trends.

Özgehan Şenyuva is Associate Professor of European Studies at the International Relations Department and the chair of European Studies Graduate Program of the Middle East Technical University, Ankara, Turkey. The Centre for European Studies of the Middle East Technical University in Ankara, Turkey was founded in 1997. It aims to contribute to comparative research on Europe and European integration through an interdisciplinary team of researchers. Through the teaching and research strengths of four academic departments at METU (International Relations, Political Science and Public Administration, Economics, and Business Administration), it offers two different Master of Science programmes in European Studies and European Integration. CES-METU became a Jean Monnet Centre of Excellence in 2007.

Róisín Smith is Senior Researcher with the Institute of International and European Affairs. She holds a PhD in Political Science from Queen's University Belfast and lectures in International Relations at Maynooth University. Róisín has also worked in the field of peace and conflict studies.
The Institute of International and European Affairs (IIEA) is Ireland's leading international affairs think tank. The IIEA is an independent, not-for-profit organisation with charitable status. The aim of the IIEA is to

provide a forum for all those interested in European Union and international affairs, to engage in debate and discussions, and to evaluate and share policy options. The IIEA is a member of TEPSA.

Andris Spruds is Director of the Latvian Institute of International Affairs. He holds the positions of Dean and Professor at Riga Stradins University.
The Latvian Institute of International Affairs (LIIA) is the oldest Latvian think tank that specializes in foreign and security policy analysis. The LIIA is an independent research institute that conducts research, develops publications and organizes public lectures and conferences related to global affairs and Latvia's international role and policies. The LIIA is a member of TEPSA.

Lars Stevenson holds a Master's degree in Political Science from Radboud University, Nijmegen, the Netherlands.
Radboud University is a public university with a strong focus on research located in Nijmegen, the Netherlands.

Natasza Styczyńska is an assistant professor at the Institute of European Studies of the Jagiellonian University. Currently, she is a researcher in two H2020 projects: Populist rebellion against modernity in twenty-first-century Eastern Europe: neo-traditionalism and neo-feudalism (POPREBEL) and EU Differentiation, Dominance and Democracy (EU3D). Her academic interests include transformation processes in Central and Eastern Europe, party politics, nationalism, populism and Euroscepticism in the CEE region.
The Institute for European Studies is a part of the Faculty of International and Political Studies at Jagiellonian University—the oldest and the leading university in Poland. The Institute is famous for its interdisciplinary approach that combines the perspectives of anthropology, economy, cultural studies, political sciences, history, law, and sociology.

Zdeněk Sychra is Associate Researcher at the Institute of International Relations Prague and an External Fellow at the Faculty of Social Studies at Masaryk University in Brno. His academic interests include the issues of European Union politics, the Economic and Monetary Union and political governance in the EU.
The Institute of International Relations Prague (IIR) is an independent public research institution which has been conducting scholarly research in the area of international relations since 1957. As an institution origi-

nally founded by the Ministry of Foreign Affairs of the Czech Republic, the IIR also provides policy analysis and recommendations. It tries to form a link between the academic world, the public and international political practice. The IIR is a member of TEPSA.

Funda Tekin is Director at the Institut für Europäische Politik, Berlin. She is Senior Research Fellow at the Centre for Turkey and EU-Studies, part of the Flying Faculty of the German-Turkish University and an advisory board member of TEPSA.
The Institute for European Politics (IEP) is a German non-profit organization dedicated to the study of European integration. IEP is a member of TEPSA.

Baldur Thorhallsson is Professor of Political Science, and Programme and Research Director at the Centre for Small States at the University of Iceland. His research focuses primarily on small state studies, European integration and Iceland's foreign policy.
The Institute of International Affairs (IIA) is a research, teaching and service institute in the field of international relations and European integration at the University of Iceland. IIA is a member of TEPSA.

Bianca Toma is Program Director of the Romanian Centre for European Policies coordinating projects related to good governance, justice and European Union (EU) affairs. She covered Brussels politics as EU affairs correspondent for the mainstream Romanian media.
The Romanian Centre for European Policies (CRPE) is one of the leading Romanian think-tanks specialized in EU affairs, with over 10 years of experience in implementing European and regional projects. The mission of the CRPE is to promote Romania as an influential leader in the development of EU agendas and policies. Another major objective is to advance the Europeanization processes in Romania and to promote European citizenship by providing expertise in various fields and by initiating or participating in public debates. CRPE is a member of TEPSA.

Boštjan Udovič is Associate Professor at the Faculty of Social Sciences of the University of Ljubljana and a Researcher at the Centre of International Relations. His main field of interests is diplomacy and the role of the political system. He is a member of the different national and international advisory bodies.
The Centre of International Relations (CIR) conducts interdisciplinary research in the fields of international relations, international economics

and international business, politics of international law, diplomacy, human rights, international organisations, and European integration. CIR is a long-standing and active member of TEPSA as well as several other international networks.

Steven Van Hecke is Associate Professor in Comparative and EU Politics at the Public Governance Institute of the KU Leuven. His research focuses on Europarties, EU institutions and European integration history.

KU Leuven is a research university based in Leuven that ranks among the best 50 universities worldwide. It has been identified as Europe's most innovative university for four years in a row by Reuters.

Viljar Veebel is a researcher at the Department of Political and Strategic Studies of the Baltic Defence College and a National Researcher for the European Council on Foreign Relations (ECFR). He has worked as an Academic Advisor for the Estonian government in the European Future Convention and as a researcher for OSCE, SIDA, Estonian Foreign Policy Institute and Eurasia Group. His main research interests include European security and defence initiatives, use of economic sanctions as a foreign policy tool, EU-Russia relations and related sanctions. In the current volume, he represents the Estonian Foreign Policy Institute.

The Estonian Foreign Policy Institute (EVI) is an independent, non-profit foundation that research focuses on the interests of regional security, European Union integration and enlargement, and developments in Russia. EVI is a member of TEPSA.

Ramūnas Vilpišauskas is Professor of the Institute of International Relations and Political Science, in Vilnius University. From 2009 to 2019 he was the Director of the Institute. In 2004–2009, he worked as a Chief Economic Policy Advisor to the President of Lithuania Valdas Adamkus. His main research interests include the political economy of European integration, policy analysis of public sector reforms and international political economy.

The Institute of International Relations and Political Science (IIRPS) at Vilnius University is one of the most prominent social sciences institutions in Eastern Europe and the Baltic region. The Institute is an academic institution specializing in social and political sciences.

Leonie Vrugtman is a researcher and project coordinator working on good governance, institutional accountability, EU accession, and violent extremism at the Institute for Democracy and Mediation (IDM). Leonie previously worked at the International Institute for Strategic Studies and the Dickson Poon School of Law in London.

IDM is an independent think tank established in Tirana in 1999, working on good governance, security sector reform, civil society development and EU integration.

Marlene Wind is Professor and the Director of the Centre for European Politics (CEP) and a Professor of Law at iCourts Centre of Excellence and the Faculty of Law, both at the University of Copenhagen. Her research is, among other things, focused on the institutional changes and treaties of the European Union, including Danish European Union policymaking and Danish opt-outs. In recent years, her research emphasis has been on the interplay between law and politics in the European Union, but also on politics and law from a more theoretical point of view.

The Centre for European Politics (CEP) is a research centre at the Department of Political Science at the University of Copenhagen. The centre was established in October 2007 and concerns itself with research within the field of European politics, particularly on the European Union.

Wouter Wolfs is Senior Research Fellow at the Public Governance Institute of the KU Leuven where he teaches comparative and international politics. His research focuses on the financing of Europarties, Euroscepticism and the role of national parliaments in the EU.

KU Leuven is a research university based in Leuven that ranks among the best 50 universities worldwide. It has been identified as Europe's most innovative university for four years in a row by Reuters.

Yuriy Yakymenko is Deputy Director General of the Razumkov Centre. The Razumkov Centre is a non-governmental think tank founded in 1994 and has united experts in the fields of economy, energy, law, political sciences, international relations, military security, land relations, sociology, history and philosophy. The Centre is a member of TEPSA.

Viktor Zamiatin is a leading expert on political and legal programmes at the Razumkov Centre.

The Razumkov Centre is a non-governmental think tank founded in 1994 and has united experts in the fields of economy, energy, law, political sciences, international relations, military security, land relations, sociology, history and philosophy. The Centre is a member of TEPSA.

List of Figures

Cyprus: A Pro-European Attitude, but Scepticism Still Holds Strong

Fig. 1   Cyprus party system continuum—reflecting positions expressed in European Parliament Elections 2019   28

The Netherlands: Playing with Fire? Dutch Political Parties Between Reluctant and Pragmatic Pro-Europeanism

Fig. 1   Positions on European integration and vote share of Dutch political parties. (Source: Populism and Political Parties Expert Survey *(POPPA)*. www.poppa-data.eu)   154

Fig. 2   Vote share of Eurosceptic parties. (Source: Parliament and Government Database (ParlGov, www.parlgov.org))   156

Albania: Will the EU's Ambiguity Lead to Euroscepticism?

Leonie Vrugtman

A North Atlantic Treaty Organization (NATO) Member State since 2009 and a European Union (EU) candidate country since 2014, Albania has transformed from Europe's most isolated country into the continent's most pro-EU country in under three decades. According to the spring 2019 Eurobarometer, approval rates for the EU remain over 80 percent at a time when Euroscepticism within the bloc is on the rise. This support is indicative of the positivity with which Albanians see their country's future membership in the EU. For them, membership is a guarantee for better opportunities, democratisation and higher living standards.

The high approval rates can also be ascribed to the unparalleled role the EU and Western countries have played in Albania's transformation. Upon the fall of communism, Albania was the largest recipient of Western aid per capita in the region. Initial ad hoc assistance evolved into more structured support for the country's democratisation efforts. EU's contributions under the Instrument for Pre-Accession Assistance alone are expected to reach €1.2 billion in the period between 2007 and 2020. Other western

---

L. Vrugtman (✉)
Institute for Democracy and Mediation—IDM, Tirana, Albania
e-mail: lvrugtman@idmalbania.org

© The Author(s) 2021
M. Kaeding et al. (eds.), *Euroscepticism and the Future of Europe*,
https://doi.org/10.1007/978-3-030-41272-2_1

donors include the US, EU Member States, and Switzerland. This support has consolidated their image to the point where Albanians have a higher trust in international organisations such as NATO, the UN and the EU, than in their own institutions. As a result, foreign diplomats play an increasingly important role and at times are asked to mediate in political crises—often by the same politicians who instigate them.

EU Criticism in Albania

In line with the popular demand, the country's main political parties are explicitly pro-European and subscribe to the idea that EU integration is the country's principal long-term objective. Such is the importance ascribed to integration by Albanians that when current president Ilir Meta created his own political enterprise in 2004, he named it the Socialist Movement for Integration.

To score political points and divert the public's attention from issues at home, political factions often utilise their respective contributions and their opponent's failures in relation to integration to sway public opinion in their favour. Meetings with high-ranking officials and endorsements from EU colleagues from the same political groups, are locally displayed as proof that Albanian politicians are hard-working and dedicated to integration.

Over the past years, the dominant topic with regards to EU accession is the unprecedented judicial reform Albania is undertaking with substantial support of the EU and the US. Key to its success are the vetting of 800 judges and prosecutors based on their professionalism, personal integrity and the integrity of their assets. To facilitate its transformative measures, the parliament unanimously approved constitutional changes that permit foreign observers to monitor its implementation. However, since then the reform has been subject to political manoeuvres and criticism aimed at undermining its success.

Central to this criticism is the slow implementation of the reform and the subsequent institutional vacuum it has created, as Albania's Constitutional Court and the High Court remain dysfunctional. The reform has also been criticised by some independent media and civil society organisations, given that a few judges and prosecutors that passed the vetting were unable to justify their assets. Some of whom have been cleared from the vetting and considered eligible to serve in the newly established

Special Anti-Corruption Prosecution Office, whose purpose is to investigate high-profile cases.

In response to these developments, some analysts question whether the country's political elite is genuinely committed to EU integration. A recent monitoring report of the vetting process claims that the country's entire political elite is sabotaging the reform, as they have "too much to lose" if the implementation of the reform fosters accountability and strengthens the rule of law. Meanwhile, the EU's criticism of the government remains subtle, an outcome the opposition has used to point out that Brussels prioritises stability over democratisation.

Enlargement Fatigue

Albania's journey towards the EU is characterised not only by slow reforms, but also by delays on the Union's front. Although a candidate country since 2014, Tirana has yet to open accession talks with Brussels, which would give a much-needed impetus to the reform agenda. The Commission recommended opening negotiations in 2018, but some Member States are reluctant to support Albania's accession at this stage. Notably, in spite of three positive recommendations by the Commission, Member States have been unable to reach a consensus so far. Instead, the decision is postponed again, this time until the EU—Western Balkans Summit in May 2020.

The unclear EU perspective is causing fatigue among a small, but vocal minority, who are starting to question Albania's enlargement prospects. To vindicate itself of responsibility, the Albanian government now claims that it has done its part by fulfilling the requirements and that the decision is now in the hands of the EU. While the 2019 European Elections provided relief in Albania and the region, the fear that Euroscepticism will continue to influence Member States in prolonging enlargement has not been vanquished.

What Can Be Done? Some Recommendations

Brussel's investment in Albania has set in motion vital reforms that can restore the public trust in local institutions. Putting a break on its enlargement perspective risks undermining and possibly reversing some of these results. Given that the justice reform is reaching a critical point, committing to the country's European future becomes even more important.

Anything short of a strong EU-presence could jeopardise the reform, the country's democratic future, and create a vacuum that can be exploited by anti-reformist individuals.

This presence can be obtained by keeping the EU perspective of Albania open, in line with the 2003 Thessaloniki Summit conclusions. Since then, the integration perspective has provided a solid basis through which the interest of Tirana and that of Brussels can materialise. To strengthen cooperation with Albania, the EU must continue working with local authorities to intensify the fight against organised crime and to combat corruption in public administration, the management of resources, and the procurement of public tenders.

Another area where the EU's contribution could become transformative is by calling for electoral reform as recommended by OSCE/ODIHR after the 2019 local elections. These reforms would help the Albanian electoral system to meet international standards, enhance the financial transparency of political parties, and foster accountability.

After all, the EU has vested political, diplomatic and economic interests in Albania, a country connected to the EU at all levels. However, the EU can extract further benefits from deepening this alliance by keeping enlargement perspective open and by pushing through a reform agenda that makes the country more attractive for EU investors.

Austria: Taking a Walk on the Wild Side

Paul Schmidt

Eurosceptic parties quickly adapt to changes in public opinion and Austrian politics is no exception here. After the Brexit referendum in the United Kingdom, the support for Austria's membership of the European Union (EU) increased further. While in April 2016—according to data of the Austria Society for European Politics—60 percent of Austrians wanted their country to stay in the EU, from July 2016 onwards the number of supporters grew to 77 percent in December 2017 and as of December 2019 stands at 75 percent. In the same period, the number of those preferring to exit the EU decreased sharply—from 31 percent (April 2016) to 23 percent (July 2016) and at present 8 percent (December 2019). The Freedom Party (FPÖ), nowadays the only relevant political force pursuing an explicit Eurosceptic agenda, which has played with the idea of organizing a similar referendum in the past rapidly recalculated. However, the change in mind came too late for the Presidential Elections of 2016, won by the green candidate Van der Bellen but just in time for a governmental coalition with the Conservative party (ÖVP) in 2017, signing up to a pro-European coalition agreement.

P. Schmidt (✉)
Austrian Society for European Politics (ÖGfE), Vienna, Austria
e-mail: paul.schmidt@oegfe.at

Fit for Government?

The migration challenge and the policy response, or sometimes the lack of it, have left their marks on Austrian politics. The coalition government of ÖVP and FPÖ polarized society. Rejected by one side for inward looking nationalistic and populist politics not driven by consensus in a county where social justice has been the hallmark since 1955. Applauded by others, who were giving credit for toughening-up on immigration, a zero-tolerance security discourse and a new reform agenda for the country. Drawing on lessons from the past, the ÖVP painstakingly avoided interference by the FPÖ in European matters, securing a smooth but rather low-key Austrian EU Council presidency in the second half of 2018. The government, however, did not shy away from treading the line between a pro-European mind-set and shallow criticism of European integration, playing to their home audience, generally pro-European, but critical regarding the functioning of the European Union. As a junior coalition partner, the FPÖ refrained from radical anti-Euro and anti-EU rhetoric in public, but certainly followed such an agenda on the constituent unit level. Yet, in government, the party also questioned the legal basis of the infringement procedures against Hungary and promoted the rejection of the global migration pact of the United Nations.

While in other European countries right-wing populist parties have only recently gained serious political weight, the FPÖ has been a part of the Austrian political landscape for more than 60 years. Over three decades the FPÖ played a rather minor role with voter support of about 5 percent of the electorate trying to conciliate its national and liberal party wing. In 1986, the party decided to pursue a more nationalistic and populist agenda leading to one electoral success after the other. The three governmental coalitions it joined all broke up before the end of the respective legislative term (in 1986, 2002, and 2019). In 2005, it was the FPÖ itself that split up and the newly founded—and today vanished—Alliance for the Future (BZÖ) continued in government with the ÖVP.

Political scandals of the FPÖ leadership were the reason why the latest Austrian coalition government fell in May 2019. In the following parliamentary elections in September, the FPÖ was heavily defeated. It lost 9.8 percentage points of its votes compared to 2017 and returned to opposition. The historical track-record of the FPÖ shows the remarkable contradictions between radical opposition and a more moderate junior coalition partner. They have proven they never were stable governments.

What Can Be Done? Some Recommendations

Eurosceptic parties might not always be strong enough to enter governments or remain in government for a full mandate, but their views increasingly enter mainstream politics.

Free movement of workers, Austria's deeply rooted stance against nuclear energy, free trade agreements, fears of an EU transfer union and most recently, questions of migration and integration were some of the topics that shaped the domestic EU discourse also leading to criticism of the Union. They all need to be addressed proactively rather than passively sitting them out. The growing attention given to European affairs, reflected by an increase in turnout in the last elections to the European Parliament of 14.4 percentage points, should be a good basis to build on.

In fact, there is much room for improving Europe's answer to globalization. Austrians expect that ways to strengthen the economic and social welfare of the people, to tackle climate change effectively, to eventually manage migration and to act globally need not only be discussed, but also decided and implemented. If not by the EU-27 then by a coalition willing to advance. At the same time, Austrians want the EU to be more than just an institution that promotes big business interests—a suspicion that sometimes can be heard.

The assumption that Austria's voice is not heard has to be contested by a more ambitious European engagement of national politics. Why not explain that the country is an essential part of the working of the Union and give more attention to its capacity to tackle problems that go far beyond national borders? Credible national politicians have to deliver on their European responsibility as many of the challenges they intend to solve do have major cross border dimensions. Their high profile on national level is an asset, which European civil servants and European parliamentarians cannot make up for. It does take political courage to discuss and defend rather than to reject and criticize. It also takes political honesty to talk about the evolution of national sovereignty and the merits of working together across borders. In the end, however, there is no major decision at the supranational level, where national representatives are not involved. This is an advantage for a rather small country and open economy, which cannot be sufficiently stressed.

The degree of public indifference in Austria regarding European politics is striking and should be given more scrutiny. Too often, the EU is perceived as far and remote. To bridge this gap, multipliers and those who have made first-hand positive experiences with EU programmes and initiatives may help. From teachers, to local politicians and the substantial number of Austrian Erasmus alumni, they all play an essential role. Focusing on structurally weak regions and inclusion is vital for the European integration to prosper and survive.

As the voting age in Austria is 16, concentrating on the younger generation is particularly important. If every prospective teacher would be made aware of the pros and cons of European integration prior to entering the classroom for the next decades, chances to make the EU more tangible and interesting to their pupils would substantially improve. If, in addition, every Erasmus alumni would tell his or her story, the curiosity for the other would then grow. A special focus should be given to vocational schools, where EU scepticism is usually widespread.

The EU too often resembles a group of nation states trying to forget what they actually signed up to and gives a fertile ground for Euroscepticism to strive. Yet, what is needed is quite the opposite: an ambitious national support for European decisions, explaining its reasons and its implications. European politics might not always be effective, but the Union is built on compromise, a characteristic Austrians know well and appreciate, and based on common values, solidarity and the rule of law. It tries to leave no one behind and aims at jointly solving the problems at hand. Injecting some potion of European spirit into national Austrian politics would indeed be beneficial—for the country and Europe alike.

Belgium: Breaking the Consensus? Eurosceptic Parties

Wouter Wolfs and Steven Van Hecke

Belgium has traditionally been characterized by a lasting permissive consensus on European integration issues. The Eurobarometer data shows that trust in European Union (EU) institutions is stronger than in national ones and the level of support for EU membership is relatively high, although slightly lower than was previously the case. In recent years, more dissonant voices have started to slowly undermine one of the pillars of its political system. Some parties—like the Flemish nationalist party New Flemish Alliance (N-VA)—have taken a more critical stance towards Europe, while traditional Eurosceptic parties—like the radical left Workers' Party of Belgium (PvdA/PTB)—have gained in popularity. Nevertheless, the overall *salience* of the EU as a political topic remains rather low in Belgium when it comes to party competition. This is partly because the 2019 European elections coincided with both the national and regional elections, resulting in little attention for EU related issues. Furthermore, the EU is neither part of the core ideology of any party; even the more Eurosceptic parties focus on different political topics.

W. Wolfs (✉) • S. Van Hecke
Public Governance Institute, KU Leuven, Leuven, Belgium
e-mail: wouter.wolfs@kuleuven.be; steven.vanhecke@kuleuven.be

The most outspoken Eurosceptic party on the left side of the political spectrum is the radical left Workers' Party of Belgium ("Partij van de Arbeid/Parti du Travail de Belgique"). The party wants to break up the current European treaties and replace them with new provisions that are focused on European solidarity and investments. As such, the party refrains from a protectionist approach, but favours the introduction of a far-reaching social policy in the entire EU. More specifically, the Workers' Party is in favour of extensive public investments in the social and environmental policy domains, and wants to reverse liberalization in several sectors, including agriculture, transport and health care. Creating a European minimum wage and a minimum pension are two of the party's main proposals. Although the party has a well-developed European political platform, the EU is not one of the focal points of the party. Due to ideological differences with other radical left parties in Europe, the Workers' Party is not involved in any transnational cooperation in a political party at European level. The 2019 elections signified a huge success for the party, as it increased its number of deputies at all levels and entered the European Parliament and the regional parliament of Flanders for the first time.

As a consequence of the growing electoral support for the radical left Workers' Party, the centre-left parties in Flanders and (in particular) Wallonia have taken a more critical position towards Europe. The Flemish socialist party ("Socialistische Partij—Anders") has become more vocal against the (economic) policy of the European Commission, and supports more fiscal harmonization in Europe, including a minimum corporate tax and the introduction of a financial transaction tax. The Walloon socialist party ("Parti Socialiste") has become even more outspoken in its criticism towards the European level. Paul Magnette, one of the leading politicians, has labelled himself as the "first Social Democratic Eurosceptic" and has led the assault on CETA, the free trade agreement with Canada. The regional parliament of Wallonia blocked the signing of the agreement which could only be ratified by Belgium after some additional concessions were made. Overall, however, the more critical attitude of the two Belgian social democratic parties mainly had to do with the direction of European policy and a lack of European integration, rather than advocating a return of competences to the national level.

On the right side of the political spectrum, the most Eurosceptic party in the Belgian political landscape has traditionally been the radical right Flemish Interest ("Vlaams Belang"). In the 2019 European Parliament elections it went in Flanders from 6.76 percent to 19.08 percent; a spectacular increase from one to three seats (out of 12). The party does not advocate a withdrawal from the EU or a total dissolution of the European project, but sees European integration primarily as a confederal, intergovernmental project focused on free trade. The party prefers to return to the situation before the Treaty of Maastricht and wants to abolish most EU institutions, including the European Parliament and the European Commission. In its communication, Flemish interest challenges a "European super state" and mainly focuses on immigration. For example, by cancelling the freedom of movement within the EU and by rejecting any further enlargement, in particular Turkey. The party has invested more resources in cooperation at the European level with like-minded parties, such as the French National Rally ("Rassemblement National"), the Austrian Freedom Party ("Freiheitliche Partei Österreichs") and the Dutch Freedom Party ("Partij voor de Vrijheid"). Overall, the EU position is only used instrumentally, as a part of the party's core business of anti-immigration.

In the last decade, the New Flemish Alliance ("Nieuw-Vlaamse Alliantie") has also taken a more critical attitude towards the EU. Still the largest Belgian party, it went down from 26.67 percent to 22.44 percent at the 2019 European Parliament elections, losing one seat but keeping three. The conservative party now presents itself as a euro*realist* political party, a middle ground between Europhiles arguing for a "European super state" and Eurosceptics that want to "destroy" the European Union. The party advocates a stronger European cooperation in economic affairs, defence, energy, transport, digital affairs and border protection, but renounces further integration in social affairs and fiscal policy, and wants to cut European expenditure on agriculture and cohesion.

When the N-VA entered Belgium's national government in 2014, the country's traditional pro-European consensus was challenged. The party has conducted a conflicting dual track policy: some politicians of the party, mostly members of the national or regional government, have taken a traditional pro-European position. Others, in particular the N-VA Members of European Parliament, have become much more vocal in their criticism towards the EU, in particular with regard to the policy of the European Central Bank and the European Commission's non-position on Catalonia. Also, divergent interests between the regional and federal levels led sometimes to inconclusive positions. Despite these growing asymmetries and the rise of Euroscepticism, former prime minister Charles Michel managed to personify the traditional Belgian pro-European attitude, unlike his predecessor Elio Di Rupo.

WHAT CAN BE DONE? SOME RECOMMENDATIONS

The EU level deserves its own election campaign and therefore the tradition of concurrent elections (regional, federal and European) should be abandoned, with regional and federal elections held separately from the European ones.

More attention should be paid to topical EU issues by political parties (and the media) to strengthen the public debate about the scope and the level of European integration.

Belgian MEPs should play a more prominent role within their respective political parties.

Media, civil society and academia should invest more efforts in emphasizing the "democratic surplus" of the EU's political system, in particular compared to the Belgian political system at the national as well as the regional level.

Belgian MEPs should become "ambassadors" for more transparency and accountability in the European Parliament, and "EU ambassadors" in Belgium to introduce European best practices (with regard to Commissioner hearings, transparency of interest representation and political finance, etc.) at the national level.

Bosnia and Herzegovina: Ethnopolitics and Hopeful Euroscepticism—No Light at the End of the European Tunnel?

Vedran Džihić

"Bosnia is close to the edge. We need Europe's help" read the Guardian headline to Aleksandar Brezar's article in May 2019. Almost 25 years after the end of the war, Bosnian citizens are trapped in a hand to mouth existence. Young people are leaving the country, poverty is high, toxic nationalism is ever-present and ethnopolitics remains the major primary technique of governance.

Dominant Bosnian political parties largely succumb to the ethnopolitical logic. Some of them, like the SNSD (Alliance of Independent Socialdemocrats) run by Dodik in the Republika Srpka, call themselves social democrats but are rather conservative and right-wing. Two others major Bosniak parties, the SDA (Party of the Democratic Action) and the Croatian HDZ (Croatian Democratic Union), are rather nationalist and conservative. Similar to the SNSD they define themselves through strong leadership and a strong will to control politics and the economy rather than through strong ideological positions. The three major ethno-political

V. Džihić (✉)
Austrian Institute for International Affairs (OIIP), Vienna, Austria
e-mail: vedran.dzihic@univie.ac.at

parties, which currently occupy almost 50 percent of seats in the House of Representative, all share a rather pragmatic position towards the European Union (EU). One could summarize this under the motto "We are for the EU-integration as long as it does not interfere in our political and economic business". Once the pressure from the EU is too high in terms of carrying out important reforms, these parties would rather retreat back to the usual way they do politics. This is through informal power networks and clientelism, accompanied by inciting fears of the respective "Other". Oppositional parties in both Republika Srpska and the Federation of Bosnia and Herzegovina do support EU integration but don't see it as their utmost political priority and as a topic that would help them to challenge the incumbent ethno-political parties. Under such circumstances, the Europeanisation was set up to change the paradigm and confront the ethnopolitics.

The promise of EU membership was from the beginning a promise for a better, but very distant, future given the length and complexity of the process. Yet, the EU conditionality has at least during the first phase of Europeanisation (from 2000 until 2005) contributed to reforms. The EU was seen as the best possible deal for the future. In this first few years, the original and very simple idea of Europeanization seemed to work out—we base the whole process on the idea that membership would be attainable within a reasonable and not too long period of time that would allow dominant political actors and parties to stake their political futures on it.

Over the course of the process, the EU slipped into the dilemma of how to manage expectations in times where the fast way to EU membership was not materializing nor resulting in tangible reforms, and this was felt by the population. It was at the same time that the EU started compromising the EU conditionality for the sake of at least some formal progress. Entrenched in ethno-politics, Bosnian politicians would continuously torpedo EU's efforts and reforms and thus make any compromise difficult. The EU would lower the standards for the sake of some minimal progress, but conditionality would erode. In the end, the main actors in Bosnia would retreat to the very well-established practice of ethnopolitics and particularism. This contributed to the rise of Euroscepticism.

The average Bosnian citizen is sceptical about Europe and has always included the feeling that membership will not materialize any time soon and that living conditions due to rapprochement with the EU will not improve. At the same time being sceptical about the EU always included the deeply rooted disappointment with Bosnian politics and politicians, and a widespread believe that when they talk and promise something this will speed up EU reforms for example if they lie.

Yet, the nominal support for the EU remained rather high. The Balkan Barometer of the Regional Cooperation Council (RCC) for 2019 shows that 47 percent of Bosnians still think EU membership would be a good thing. 31 percent say that it would be neither good nor bad and in comparison with the beginning of the EU integration process in 2000, it is striking that 17 percent of Bosnians believe that the EU membership would be a bad thing. Generally, there is higher support for the EU among Bosnian Croats and Bosniaks than Bosnian Serbs.

The French decision to block the start of EU accession talks with North Macedonia and Albania has produced profound uncertainty in the region and scepticism about the honesty and commitment of the EU and particularly France. The decision has furthermore emboldened anti-European and obstructionist forces all across the region and endangered ongoing reforms. The support for the EU will probably go down further. The "hopeful Euroscepticism", as I would define the phenomenon, is what is left. While the majority of the people in Bosnia see Europe as their fate and believe that there is no alternative to Europe, they do not see the European light at the end of the Bosnian tunnel materializing any time soon.

What Can Be Done? Some Recommendations

Unfortunately, there is no indication whatsoever that EU-rope in its present stage and shape is capable of being and becoming the decisive factor in the Bosnian internal arena. Are there any paths to change it? In times of stalled EU integration, I see two possible ways to bring substantial Europeanisation and democratization of societies in the future:

One way would be to embrace deep democratic reforms at home initiated by new progressive and anti-nationalist political forces and try in parallel to implement sectoral reforms (in education, transport, free travel trade across the region, and in science, etc.) supported by the EU (possible by structural funds).

The other one is to be heard and seen on the European level by joining relevant EU debates on the future of Europe. The whole region and Bosnia in particular are in dire need of a new European start, but there are no quick fixes to this complex problem.

Bulgaria: Creeping EU-Scepticism—The Tacit Consent that Fuels Populism

Hristo Panchugov and Ivan Nachev

The political turmoil of the early 90s saw unstable and short-lived governments, culminating in a political crisis in 1997. A new Union of Democratic Forces (UDF), pro-democratic and pro-European Government, firmly established the European Union (EU) perspective as the dominant paradigm in society. As a result, in the beginning of the twenty-first century the citizens of Bulgaria were extremely Europositive. The first year of EU membership saw that 78 percent of Bulgarians had positive attitudes towards the EU. Only 10 percent thought that the membership was bringing more negatives than positives. Some reminiscence of the anti-North Atlantic Treaty Organization (NATO) and Euroscepticism still could be found within the attitudes and the electorate of the Bulgarian Socialist Party (BSP). However, along the lines of issues with regards to the history of North Macedonia and protecting Bulgarian energy sector, both were fuelled by the pro-Russian sentiments within the BSP.

However, this is no longer the case and the Bulgarian society has started to doubt the benefits of its membership in the Union. While in the wake of the 2019 EP elections, 51 percent of the respondents believe in the

H. Panchugov (✉) • I. Nachev
New Bulgarian University, Sofia, Bulgaria
e-mail: h.panchugov@gmail.com; e-mail: ivannachevbg@gmail.com

positives of Bulgaria membership in the EU and 54 percent support further integration with the EU, 45 percent believe there should be more power transferred to national states. 66 percent of the Bulgarians do not feel that they are citizens of the EU. At a more detailed view only 36 percent believe the voice of Bulgaria is being heard in the EU, against 49 percent thinking otherwise. 30 percent approve the work of the EU leaders, while 49 percent do not approve it. A playing field which is very susceptible to populist and Eurosceptic influences, especially considering the fact that 61 percent do not approve the EU migration policy.

The change started in 2001 with the arrival of the last Bulgarian monarch Simeon II, and the founding of his party National Movement Simeon II—NDSV. The party won on populism and charisma, but the movement never really started its ideological institutionalization, setting up the common trend for the upcoming parties. The vacuum was created by its demise and the gradual shift of BSP towards a favourable stance on the EU, which opened up a space for nationalist and populist parties.

The first Eurosceptic party to enter the Parliament in 2005 was "Attack". Mixing elements taken from national-socialism and its pro-Russian and anti-NATO positions, the party adopted a moderate stance on EU membership due to the enormous support that the EU had in Bulgarian society (the figures above). Populist and nationalistic discourses gradually became the playfield of the newcomer political parties. GERB was established in 2006, largely on the personal charisma and the anti-establishment message delivered by the party Leader Boyko Borisov. Forming minority governments in 2009 and 2014, GERB relied on the tacit support of Attack. This initiated the creeping legitimization of nationalism and Euroscepticism in the mainstream politics. The number of Eurosceptic parties increased with the Patriotic Front (NFSB and IMRO) entering the parliament in 2014 and the new populist party "Will" in 2017. These four parties amounted for the largest representation of Eurosceptics in the Bulgarian Parliament.

As a result, Boyko Borisov's third government (2017) was formed in coalition with the United Patriots, thus publicly legitimizing xenophobic, anti-immigration, anti-NATO and Eurosceptical parties. Scandals related to abuse of power, public procurement, European funds and corruption further characterized the government. Thus, GERB's ruling coalition erodes and disrupted confidence in the EU. This moved the country away from Schengen and the eurozone and in the long run, strengthened anti-European sentiments.

Since 2007 the nationalist parties have a permanent presence in the European Parliament with 3 MEPs in 2007, 2 in both 2009 and 2014. BSP has undertaken a major move towards Eurosceptic and pro-Russian positions. Along with the United Patriots it has led the debate against immigration and lifting sanctions against Russia. Due to the low turnout and the "radicalization" of BSP and winning 5 MEPs, IMRO won 2 MEPs, while receiving two times less votes. The Eurosceptic narrative revolved around Emmanuel Macron's new transport initiative, migration, gender issues and the low standard of living. This was all explained with the double standards of the EU and these claims have been legitimized by the government decision to withdraw Bulgaria from the Istanbul Convention and its officially adopted stance on the double quality standards in the Union.

In this context, the passive role of the European Commission and the support of the European People's Party (EPP) for what is perceived to be a corrupt government is not understood by the Bulgarian citizens. The ambiguous position of the EPP regarding Viktor Orban's membership and the lack of sanctions for his party's behaviour has given legitimacy to the claims that the illiberal democracy is the future.

The general lack of trust in Bulgarian institutions is as low as 8 percent in the National Parliament and 15 percent in the Government. This undermines the credibility of democracy and the EU. The political apathy, lack of participation and perception of the lack of alternative were dominating the EP elections.

Still, the success of Eurosceptic parties in the EP elections shows that no real change of the Government's EU policy influences national politics and has been significantly higher and out of proportion in showing support. This is because Pro-European parties still hold 15 of the 17 seats in the EP.

Overall the rise of Eurosceptic populism and nationalistic sentiments can be attributed to the following factors:

1. The success and willingness to use of anti-establishment, anti-systemic rhetoric can attribute to the success of the newcomer parties after 2001.
2. Diminishing, as a result of populism, public support for the institutions and politics in general, in Bulgaria.
3. Legitimating the nationalistic rhetoric and its proponents through their inclusion in Government; tacitly after 2005, and directly in 2017.

4. The ambiguous role of the EU parties' families in relation to the protection of the fundamental values the EU is based upon.
5. The absence of an active role of the EU Commission in the national debates on controversial topics in relation to the EU versus national sovereignty.

What Can Be Done? Some Recommendations

As long as these are not tackled the situation might further aggravate these developments. Consequently, the following recommendations can be made:

Active opposition on behalf of the main European party families to accommodate ambiguous and straightforward anti-democratic sentiments and behaviour practiced by different national members of the party alliances.

Filing the vacuum in the debate concerning the EU as the guardian of freedom and democracy is a must. The Commission and the EU need a new face! An identifiable and clear stance and active engagement on any issues that fuels anti-EU and anti-democratic sentiments.

Adopting active "naming and shaming" practice in relation to behaviour that goes against the fundamental values of the EU and democratic government.

Croatia: The Government Should Take Citizens Seriously

Hrvoje Butković

Since the accession of Croatia into the European Unions (EU) in 2013, the country has gone through one regular parliamentary election in 2015 and one that was irregular in 2016 as well as one major government reconstruction in 2017. The background behind much of this political volatility was Euroscepticism which since the EU accession became embraced by a number of new political parties.

In 2015, the ruling socialists lost power to a new conservative majority. However, the centre right pro-EU Croatian Democratic Union (HDZ) was unable to form a government without a far right and Eurosceptic junior partner MOST. The irregular elections of 2016 happened after a change of leadership within HDZ which positioned the party closer to the political centre. However, the coalition with MOST was tried again, only to be dissolved in mid-2017 when MOST was replaced by liberals. This stabilised the government internally but left behind a bitter taste of voters' betrayal. The liberals in Croatia are considered a left wing party and they

H. Butković (✉)
Institute for Development and International Relations, Zagreb, Croatia
e-mail: hrvoje.butkovic@irmo.hr

© The Author(s) 2021
M. Kaeding et al. (eds.), *Euroscepticism and the Future of Europe*,
https://doi.org/10.1007/978-3-030-41272-2_6

won their parliamentary seats in a pre-election coalition with the socialists. The unexpected coalition between the centre right HDZ and the liberals left many of their voters frustrated.

The level of voters' dissatisfaction with the government became evident from the results of the 2019 EP elections. The ruling Croatian Democratic Union (HDZ) and the strongest opposition Social Democratic Party (SDP), which are both pro-EU parties, won four seats each out of a total of 12 seats allocated to Croatia. The remaining four seats were obtained by the Eurosceptic far-right Sovereigntist Coalition, the liberal pro-EU Amsterdam Coalition, the Eurosceptic far-left Human Shield Party and an independent Eurosceptic candidate Mislav Kolakušić.

These results were considered a disaster for the ruling HDZ, which with 22.7 percent of votes obtained in the worst election result since its foundation 30 years ago. The combined percentages obtained by the Eurosceptic far-right (21.9 percent) and the far-left (13.4 percent) parties and candidates were an incredible 35.3 percent. Regardless, of the fact that only three such lists managed to win more than 5 percent of the votes and thereby secured seats in the EP. Compared with results of 2016 national elections, the Eurosceptic candidates increased their support by a staggering 18 percent. If this trend persists in the future the only possibility for avoiding the Eurosceptic parties in the government will be a grand coalition between HDZ and SDP.

The successes of the Eurosceptic parties call for an evaluation of the government's policies, since 2016 when the HDZ started to be led by the Prime Minister Andrej Plenković. He often insisted upon implementation of politically sensitive actions that were supported by the EU but simultaneously lacked popular support in Croatia. One such action that tumbled upon much opposition concerns the program of introducing the Euro in Croatia initiated in late 2017. The opponents of this program among political parties and trade unions acknowledged the fact that the EU encourages all countries that satisfy the economic criteria to join the eurozone. However, they argued that Croatia should not rush this because only some 40 percent of citizens approve introducing the Euro at this moment. Furthermore, other non-eurozone Member States currently seem hesitant about making this step.

Similarly, in January 2019 the pension reform was adopted which raised the retirement age from 65 to 67 and cut pensions for those who retired early. Responding to this EU inspired reform in the early 2019 three trade union federations launched their campaign to call the referendum which would cancel this reform. After securing all formal prerequisites for the referendum in September 2019 the government, fearing its outcome, decided to comply with all trade union demands.

Backsliding in combating corruption represents an additional factor behind the growing success of the Eurosceptic parties and candidates. After the EU accession a certain backsliding in the anticorruption efforts was recorded within various rating reports. Particularly troubling is the pattern of higher courts overturning major corruption convictions on procedural grounds. The issue is closely linked to Croatia's EU membership because the fight against corruption was in the centre of transformation efforts during the EU accession. The citizens expected less corruption after the EU accession which did not happen, and many became disillusioned with the EU.

What Can Be Done? Some Recommendations

The presented analysis indicates that forming post-election alliances between parties that were bitter opponents during the election time fuels voters' dissatisfaction and ultimately Euroscepticism. Concerning the EU inspired reforms such as fast introduction of the Euro or increasing the retirement age a polarizing tension could be observed. On one side there is the Euro-optimistic government and the business community that support such actions, while on the other there is a growing number of citizens which oppose them, fearing possible economic consequences. In both cases the government fostered a one-sided debate that emphasized the benefits and downsized potential problems, which only strengthened the Eurosceptic sentiment. This shows that popular opposition cannot be taken lightly, and that government needs to engage in detailed, honest and plural discussions about the consequences of such far reaching actions.

The citizens' frustration with corruption seems to be a driving force behind much of the Eurosceptic rhetoric. Therefore, the government should fight corruption with much more rigor, delivering concrete results. The EU for its part needs to develop a post-accession conditionality mechanism related to the state of anti-corruption efforts in its Member States. Backsliding in this area should be sanctioned by concrete measures such as limiting the access to EU funds.

Cyprus: A Pro-European Attitude, but Scepticism Still Holds Strong

Giorgos Kentas

Euroscepticism is on demise in Cyprus. The Spring Eurobarometer in 2019 shows that Cypriots' trust in the European Union (EU) has increased by 13 percent. It is now the majority view with 54 percent; this is 10 percent above the EU average. Public perceptions however are but one facet of the political spectrum and equal attention must be paid to the party system. Currently, the Government, which is led by the Democratic Rally (DISY), has a pro-Europeanist approach. In addition to DISY, the Parliament includes seven opposition parties, the leftist AKEL, the centrist DIKO, the social-democratic EDEK, Solidarity (Allilegi), Citizen's Alliance (Symmaxia Politon), the Ecologists (Oikologoi), and the ethnonationalist ELAM. When party positions are put together, one may discern a pro-European attitude to prevail, but pockets of scepticism still hold strong.

G. Kentas (✉)
Departments of Politics and Governance, School of Law, University of Nicosia, Nicosia, Cyprus
e-mail: kentas.g@unic.ac.cy

A Pro-Europeanist Trend?

According to the latest Eurobarometer, Cypriots appear optimistic for the future of the EU by 65 percent. Equally, 62 percent believes that its voice counts in the EU and the democratic processes in the Union are more positively approached compared to a year ago.

Three more findings add to a pro-Europeanist trend. First, seven out of ten respondents feel like citizens of the EU. This positions Cypriots among the three-quarters of respondents at EU level. Second, there is strong support for economic and monetary union with one single currency, the euro with 74 percent. Third, there is an equally strong support for the free movement of EU citizens who can live, work, study, and do business anywhere in the EU with 88 percent.

This positive development must have an explanation. During the period the survey was contacted in June/July 2019, EU officials, that is, Mr. Tusk, Mr. Juncker, and Ms. Mogherini, expressed strong solidarity in supporting the Republic of Cyprus vis-à-vis Turkey's illegal activities in the Republic's exclusive economic zone. A second explanation pertains to the new confidence of Cypriots toward the future of their country in the EU and euro-area after a tough economic crisis. Last but not least, the positive image of the EU is prevalent across both the Greek and Turkish Cypriots. This demonstrates an embedded trust in the Union. On the other hand, the low turnout in the European Parliament elections (44.99 percent) begs for a much deeper inquiry into citizens' perceptions.

Party Politics and Governmental Orientation

Europeanism in Cyprus went through some fluctuations. In the early 1990s, there was a pro-Europeanist turn and after 1993 when European Commission issued a positive Avis for Cyprus the sceptic political parties abandoned reservations for EU membership which dated back to the 1970s. AKEL (GUE/NGL affiliated), the second-largest party, and EDEK (S&D affiliated), the fourth-largest party, thought that EU membership would have a positive impact on the Cyprus problem. Traditional pro-European parties, DISY (EPP affiliated), the largest party, and DIKO (S&D affiliated), the third-largest party, were behind EU membership but maintained lofty expectations on what the Union may offer to Cyprus.

EU accession re-opened the debate and eurozone membership was the first test. AKEL was the only party to express severe scepticism on euro-area. All other parties supported the adoption of the euro and the economic and monetary requirements it entailed. EDEK shifted preferences and joined DISY and DIKO in supporting euro-area accession while AKEL argued for delaying membership.

That first post-accession debate showed some strong signs of pro-Europeanism. A couple of years later when Cyprus entered a vicious circle of financial and sovereign crisis, the political spectrum was again restructured. For the first time, the economy topped the agenda. Cyprus joined the EU with strong economic statistics and optimism for an even better performance in the euro-area. Good macroeconomic figures of 2006–2008 were soon overturned to reveal some problematic public finances. AKEL-led Government (2008–2013) was reluctant in resorting to European institutions for an adjustment program. It did not adopt a national program to restructure public finances. Instead it opted for a Russian loan to deal with short-term needs. The crisis however was structural and could not be addressed with ad-hoc solutions.

Events leading to a EC/ECB/IMF-sponsored Adjustment Program and the March 2013 dramatic Eurogroup decision were based on Cyprus' Government recommendation for a bail-in arrangement in the banking sector. That outturn yielded a new dichotomy in the party system that holds strong even today. DISY and DIKO, although regretted the unfortunate bail-in, committed in implementing the Adjustment Program. All other parties stood firmly against that program, however without presenting an alternative. That situation cultivated a new form of Euroscepticism, one that holds EU responsible for a harsh adjustment program that had negative economic and financial implications for the middle and lower classes.

Across the party system, Euroscepticism is mostly fuelled by two issues: firstly, a critique of the Union's impact on the Cyprus problem. The EU membership united all parties in a pro-European campaign in anticipation of a settlement in line with Union standards. Weak EU impact on the settlement process generates scepticism. Secondly, in the post-economic crisis era there is more systematic scrutiny of EU socio-economic policies. Sceptic parties exert less confidence on the impact of these policies and tend to criticize them for failing to address citizens' needs.

Scepticism on EU's impact on the Cyprus problem appears across the party system. Socio-economic scepticism appeals more to some parties than to others. European elections campaign in 2019 offered a good opportunity for a closer understating of the party system in the pro-Europeanism vs Euroscepticism continuum (Fig. 1).

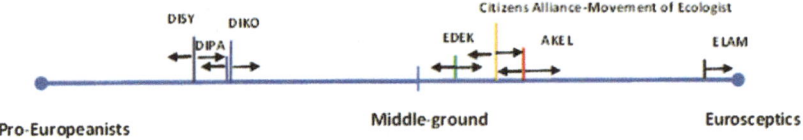

Fig. 1 Cyprus party system continuum—reflecting positions expressed in European Parliament Elections 2019

The darkest face of Euroscepticism in Cyprus is associated with ELAM. That party enjoyed growing support in consecutive elections. Some expected to have won even a seat in European Parliament. Recent estimations present ELAM on the wane and the next Parliament elections in 2021 shall be a crucial test.

What Can Be Done? Some Recommendations

Having identified the main sources of Euroscepticism in historic and contemporary times, some recommendations are considered for taming the phenomenon. The basis to begin with is an emerging pro-Europeanist trend at the grassroots. The Government needs to collaborate closely with EU institutions, academia, and NGOs for initiating more effective communication programs. Scepticism must be addressed through information campaigns as some surveys reveal a deficit of knowledge. The more citizens learn about the EU, the more they will understand about it, and the more they will be empowered to interact with institutions, and in turn the more they will seek and enjoy the benefits.

Scepticism is not malign when the quest is the improvement of the Union. But Euroscepticism is a convenient choice for parties that appeal on popular sentiments and is a means of political comfort to the ill-intentioned and those who mean to hurt the EU rather than help it. In that regard, local pro-European actors need to reveal and expose ill intentions and channel debate to political propositions that would improve the Union.

Cypriots know for sure that there is no alternative to the EU in seeking the best possible future for their country. This is the strongest political predisposition to promote pro-Europeanism and channel scepticism to creativeness, away from rejectionism.

Czechia: Who Is the Most Eurosceptic of Them All? The Eurosceptic Race to the Bottom

Zdeněk Sychra and Petr Kratochvíl

EUROSCEPTIC PARTIES, EUROSCEPTIC PUBLIC

Any discussion on Euroscepticism in Czechia has to face the uncomfortable truth that Euroscepticism is omnipresent in political debates, in the media and in the broader public sphere. Paradoxically, there are not many Czech parties that would call themselves Eurosceptic and those who would call for a Czexit are even fewer. Having said this, the entire political spectrum has shifted towards a generalized Euroscepticism during the last fifteen years. It is not uncommon even for the mainstream political parties to borrow the language of hard Eurosceptics and the distrust towards

---

Z. Sychra (✉)
Department of International Relations and European Studies, Faculty of Social Studies, Masaryk University, Brno, Czech Republic
e-mail: sychra@fss.muni.cz

P. Kratochvíl
Institute of International Relations Prague, Prague, Czech Republic
e-mail: kratochvil@iircz.onmicrosoft.com

© The Author(s) 2021
M. Kaeding et al. (eds.), *Euroscepticism and the Future of Europe*,
https://doi.org/10.1007/978-3-030-41272-2_8

"Brussels unelected bureaucrats" permeates every aspect of Czech public debate. The two most recent Czech Presidents Václav Klaus and Miloš Zeman are both epitomes of Czech Euroscepticism. While the former was once a neoliberal and the latter a Social Democrat, they have gradually become indistinguishable in this respect as their critique of the EU has gained increasingly ultraconservative and nationalist overtones.

The resulting distribution of Czech political parties across the Eurosceptic-Eurooptimistic spectrum is threefold: (1) hard Eurosceptic parties, (2) mainstream parties with strongly EU-critical elements and (3) pro-European parties. Only three smaller parties in the fragmented Lower House of the Czech Parliament can be described as purely Eurosceptic. The oldest of these are the Communists (KSČM). Their support has been steadily declining (7.8 percent in the 2017 parliamentary elections), but their political importance—thanks to their support of the coalition minority government—is still disproportionately large. On the right, the strongest anti-European entity is the Direct Democracy Party (SPD, 10.6 percent), a xenophobic, nationalist movement with racist undertones. The third subject is the small, yet growing Tricolour movement, represented by only two deputies who broke away from the Civic Democratic Party (ODS) club.

Among the parties that are distrustful of the EU are the dominant ANO movement (which gained around 30 percent of the votes in the last national elections) and the strongest opposition party, the conservative ODS (11.3 percent of the votes). While for the latter, Euroscepticism is more of a long-term ideological stance, the ANO movement of Prime Minister Andrej Babiš is a more complex case. The Prime Minister's criticism of the EU is primarily aimed at the domestic audience, while the movement seeks to act as a constructive actor abroad. Finally, there are several broadly pro-European parties: The Pirate Party (10.8%) and four smaller parties—the Social Democrats (ČSSD), the Christian Democrats (KDU-ČSL), the liberal conservative TOP 09 and the Mayors and Independents (STAN) movement.

Four general trends thus define Czech Euroscepticism: the gradual shift of the entire political spectrum towards a more Eurosceptic attitude, the emergence of an endless series of small, radical Eurosceptic movements, the continued crisis of the old pro-European parties (the Social Democrats and TOP 09) and, most recently, the emergence of non-traditional progressive pro-European groupings on both the national and municipal level, of which the Pirate Party is the strongest. The 2019 European elections confirmed all four of these developments as almost all the parties that succeeded in the national elections won seats in the European Parliament. The ANO movement was again victorious in these elections but its six European Parliament seats out of the Czech Republic's 21 can hardly be considered a great success. The soft Eurosceptic, but increasingly conservative ODS gained slightly more seats than it had previously (four seats). The Pirates scored three seats, and the coalition of two other EU-friendly parties (TOP 09 and STAN) gained three seats as well. The only major difference compared to the national election was the failure of the pro-European Social Democrats, who did not win a single seat in the European Parliament elections.

Taken together, this political situation and the state of the national public sphere also explain the negative attitudes of Czechs towards the EU. According to the Eurobarometer, from Spring 2019, the Czech belong to the most Eurosceptic people in almost every conceivable dimension. Only 36 percent trust the EU, and they are among the least optimistic groups regarding the EU's future, and only 58 percent feel European citizens (which puts them on par with the Brexiting UK).

THE IMPACT OF EUROSCEPTICS ON CZECH EU POLICIES? ONLY A LIMITED ONE

Given the prevalence of Eurosceptic attitudes among the public as well as in many political parties, it may sound surprising that this rhetoric has had only a limited impact on Czech EU policies. The Communists, who support the current Czech minority government, belong to the very EU-critical wing of the Czech political spectrum and yet, their contribution to the EU-related debates is reactive, feeble and ineffective. What has, however, influenced the Czech official position is the dominant position of the ANO movement. Following the party's victory in the 2017 election, ANO's chairman and subsequently the Czech Prime Minister Andrej Babiš has been walking the narrow line between critical rhetoric for domestic consumption and the more constructive approach he utilizes in Brussels. The Prime Minister's rhetoric is partially offset by the Social Democratic Foreign Minister as well as the ANO MEPs, who are much more pro-European than their party leader.

But the overall trend is unmistakable: Czech EU policy is becoming more and more critical towards the EU, and those who once simply preferred intergovernmental cooperation over federalization are now more or less openly nationalistic. The debate about the EU migration policy and particularly the migrant relocation scheme constituted a turning point and after the crisis, it has become common to perceive the EU as a meddling great power that imposes its will on the smaller nations, with some politicians even claiming that we are witnessing a second Munich Agreement. This critique often then very easily spills over to other policy domains: The introduction of the common currency is almost universally rejected and so is the deepening of the eurozone. The previous European Commission became a target of much of this critique, with Jean Claude Juncker a particularly hated figure.

The single biggest policy result is the even stronger alignment and identification of the country with the Visegrad Group. The Group is often depicted as the last safe haven for Czechs and the only platform where Czech interests are taken seriously. This is all the more paradoxical given the declining state of democracy in Hungary and Poland, for whom the Czechs play the role of useful advocates within the EU, while also tarnishing themselves with Visegrad's bad reputation. As a result, the EU is largely seen as a hostile external actor rather than as part of the Czech identity.

What Can Be Done? Some Recommendations

First and foremost, Czech diplomacy should stop using the Visegrad Group as the main vehicle for the promotion of Czech interests in the EU. The overall authoritarian turn in the Group combined with the all-permeating critique of the EU is harmful in terms of the Czech perceptions of the Union as well as in terms of broader coalition building.

Instead, the Government should finally define the country's long-term goals in the EU, but also clearly spell out its vision for the future of the EU which would be both democratic and efficient. These goals should be pursued within a wide range of flexible coalitions of like-minded countries, which is clearly the winning strategy used by a number of other member states.

Building on this reorientation of its EU policy, the Government should radically redefine its communication strategy. The current purely utilitarian arguments can never lead to a shift in the public perceptions of the integration process. In a similar manner, the dominant framing of the EU as a threat, rather than an opportunity, should be abandoned.

Changing the communication strategy is not enough, however. The Government should also start to seriously address those concerns of Czech Eurosceptics that are rooted in the fears of socio-economic decline as well as political marginalization.

Denmark: Ambivalence Towards the EU—From Foot-Dragging to Pacesetters?

Maja Kluger Dionigi and Marlene Wind

Euroscepticism appears to be running out of steam in Denmark. Danish voters' attitudes towards European Union (EU) membership has peaked in 2019 with 75 percent seeing it as a good thing. This is only the second highest score across the EU in Eurobarometer polls, and is only surpassed by Germany. Danish voters are also the second most optimistic about the EU after Ireland. Polling suggests that Euroscepticism is losing ground in Denmark as a consequence of Britain's vote for Brexit.

The Danes' mood towards the EU is changing but not dramatically.

On the surface, there seems to be a mood change in Denmark. The Danes' support for EU membership has increased. The tremendous blow suffered by the once influential Eurosceptic parties in both the European Parliament (EP) and the Danish general elections of 2019 corroborate the Danish mood change.

M. Kluger Dionigi
Think Tank Europa, Copenhagen, Denmark
e-mail: mkr@thinkeuropa.dk

M. Wind (✉)
Centre for European Politics, Copenhagen, Denmark
e-mail: mwi@ifs.ku.dk

Contrary to the overall European dynamics, Danish Eurosceptic parties have performed poorly, and mainstream parties have maintained their mandates or at least increased them in the 2019 EP election. The high turnout of 66 percent was another surprise that exceeded most expectations, especially with first-time voters and young citizens boosting the turnout, as it has never been so high before for EP elections.

The most remarkable development is no doubt that the Danish People's party (DPP, Dansk Folkeparti) lost three of its seats in the EP election and arrived fourth among Danish parties compared to the first position it had five years ago. A lot probably has to do with the 'Meld & Feld' fraud case on misuse of funds from the EP. Two other Eurosceptic parties, the libertarian Liberal Alliance and the People's Movement against the EU (Folkebevægelsen mod EU), did not gain any representation and the latter left out after 40 years in the EP. Unlike the general EU trend, Danish mainstream parties fared well and the Liberals (Venstre) came first and won 4 seats (the fourth seat to be taken up after Brexit) and the Social Democrats (Socialdemokratiet) maintained its three seats and came second.

Ten days later, the Danish general election followed a similar pattern. DPP lost 21 of its 37 mandates. In one of the most epic collapses in Danish election history in a Parliament (Folketinget) with a total of 179 seats. The Liberal Alliance lost two-thirds of its seats and its leader went from the role of foreign minister to leave politics altogether because he simply was not re-elected.

One should not, however, be fooled by Denmark's apparent pro-European appearance. The Eurosceptic parties may have lost votes, but the DPP has heavily influenced both the Danish Liberals and Social Democrats, the two largest Danish parties, over the past two decades. The Liberals lost the general election after it was outfoxed by the Social Democrats on taking its immigration policy further to the right and toning down its pro-EU rhetoric. According to the Dutch populism researcher Cas Mudde, the 'taking in' of the positions of the far right has in fact gone further in Denmark than anywhere else in Europe. In his new book 'The Far Right Today', he argues that one of the most prevalent signs of this is that it is considered almost absurd to even question the political legitimacy of the far right today in the Danish public debate.

The Danes' EU support may have reached historically high levels, but a large segment of the population still opposes sovereignty transfers and sees a close link between having opt-outs and safeguarding sovereignty. There are no prospects of abolishing any of the Danish EU opt outs anytime soon.

Unlike the previous centre right government, the Social Democrats do not support a referendum on the defence opt-out (or any of the other opt-outs concerning justice and home affairs and the Euro). The Liberals are divided on whether or not Denmark should join the banking union. The Social Democrats have not yet made up their mind but are in favour of holding a referendum before joining even though it is not legally required. Current opinion polls do not show a majority in favour of joining the banking union.

The Liberals and Social Democrats agree when it comes to the issue of keeping Denmark's temporary border control with Germany despite the lack of evidence that it is working, which is in many ways a copy pasting of the DPP's policies. Moreover, the Social Democrats recently joined forces with the DPP by backing the introduction of border control with Sweden in November 2019.

The Danes view the EU as an excellent cooperation as long as it does not interfere too much with our perceived 'sovereignty' and the Danish way of doing things (e.g. our opt-outs and welfare state). For instance, most of the Danes and political establishment are against EU proposals that interfere with the Danish contractual model between employers and employees in the labour market, such as a minimum wage. Interestingly, for this reason Denmark was recently against the so-called 'work-life-balance' directive, which is to secure 2 months paid parental leave to men. However, even though one might have thought that this was something Denmark would have supported, Denmark was voted down in the Council. This, thus, sends some mixed and rather conservative signals, which was reflected in Denmark's negative approach to the EU's new social pillar, which other Nordic countries have embraced. In other areas, such as further deepening the single market and improving the EU's environmental and climate legislation, the Danes want the EU to do more.

Brexit seems to have been a wake-up call for Denmark in terms of increasing the support for EU-membership, but it has also fuelled concerns about Denmark's voice in Europe. With Brexit, Denmark stands to lose a close cooperation partner and an important 'bridge' (the UK) to other Member States. In fact a recent study by the European Council of Foreign Relations measuring EU 'member state-connectedness', showed that none of the other Member States saw Denmark as their most important partner (though Denmark had pointed at Sweden and Germany as its most important EU-ally). In other words, the Social Democratic government continues its effort to find new alliances one of them being within 'the Hanseatic League 2.0'. The government still has the view that the EU should be trade-focused and stay clear of centralisation and grandiose (Macron-inspired) ambitions of major reforms. Denmark, thereby, signals that it holds a firm foot on the EU's integration brakes (even without the dependence of the DPP) and remains hesitant to relinquish powers to Brussels when it touches upon core state powers.

What Can Be Done? Some Recommendations

The most important thing to do to acquire new allies would be to start taking more initiatives at the European level. Being proactive not only in the usual areas but also when it comes to issues that really concern people like tax fraud and fighting American tax giants. This is something that Denmark, with its Commissioner Margrethe Vestager, has become increasingly associated with. It will also be important to stop being so negative when it comes to a common European minimum wage and the EU's social pillar. A lot will happen in this area in the future and it's time that the Danish government starts listening a bit less to cooperate interests in Denmark (who fight to prevent any change in this area) and more at how the single market might benefit from a less conservative Danish view.

All in all, it will be essential for Danish influence and attractiveness as someone to 'do business with' in the years ahead that Denmark becomes more proactive. At least if it sincerely wants to escape its current role and reputation as a Member State that primarily reacts to proposals and ideas from others.

Estonia: Challenges with the Popularity of Right-Wing Radicalism

Viljar Veebel

Since joining the North Atlantic Treaty Organization (NATO) and the European Union (EU) in 2004, Estonia has been an exemplar of rationality and democratic values, becoming an epitome of digital innovation, openness and budgetary balance. This can be exemplified by looking at the peak of the global financial crisis in 2008, when Estonia quickly took austerity measures to overcome the crisis, setting a model for other states in the EU. Despite painful reforms and budgetary constraints, Estonia's liberal and conservative political parties retained their popularity. For nearly two decades, a liberal social consensus existed: with each year of independence, Estonians expected that their civil society and democratic institutions would continue to grow stronger.

Then, fracturing the flawless image, an unexpected change occurred in 2014–2015. A previously marginal anti-European populist party, the Conservative People's Party of Estonia (EKRE), started gaining popularity. In 2010, support for EKRE stood around 2–3 percent. In July 2019 it fluctuated around 20 percent. The reasons for this dramatic arise is that there appeared a wider social dissatisfaction with the policies of previous

---

V. Veebel (✉)
Baltic Defence College, Tartu, Estonia
e-mail: Viljar.Veebel@ut.ee

© The Author(s) 2021
M. Kaeding et al. (eds.), *Euroscepticism and the Future of Europe*,
https://doi.org/10.1007/978-3-030-41272-2_10

coalition parties. They had become more and more blind or ineffective toward some social problems (inner and outer migration, sovereignty and economic sustainability) or groups (farmers, people with lower income, etc). Next to these specific aspects, the rise of radical right-wing popularity was supported from a wider growth of popularity of radical and anti-European parties in Central and East Europe.

In 2019 parliamentary elections, EKRE delivered the third-best result, defeating many traditional parties, such as the left-leaning Social Democrats and the conservative Pro Patria. EKRE's strong result allowed it not only to join the governing coalition but also to become the dominant voice in dictating the political agenda. This was possible due to the combination of strong mutual mistrust between the former coalition members (Reform Party, Social Democrats and the Centre Party) and hunger for capturing the prime-minister position between two winning parties of 2019 parliamentary election; Reform Party and the Centre Party. This political change was not caused by any economic woes or by mistrust towards the EU. Estonia has an average economic growth of roughly 4 percent since 2016 and Eurobarometer surveys from 2019 show that trust in the EU is reaching to 69 percent, after a slight decline during the 2015 refugee crisis (which drove the initial popularity of EKRE).

Ideologically, EKRE descends from Estonia's ethno-nationalist rural movement, which emerged during the so-called Singing Revolution that led Estonia to regain independence in the early 1990s. Curiously, institutionally, electorally and in terms of party membership, it also relies on the former Soviet collective farms related circles. In its yearning for the lost paradise, the ethnic imagery coalesces with the lost Soviet overpaid agricultural sector. Yet, ideologically, it does not attempt to rebuild the Soviet system. Rural roots, predominantly free-market economics, and clear anti-Russian attitudes differentiate EKRE from many other anti-EU radical parties in Europe.

EKRE's message is that the local political elite—"the establishment"—restricts the sovereignty of ordinary Estonians, and proclaims that EKRE is the only Estonian political party protecting them. EKRE criticizes traditional liberal institutions (such as courts and universities), European integration, the media, and minorities and foreigners simultaneously. As a result, the party's rhetoric is often confusing and illogical. On top of this, EKRE's—now a leading partner in the national government and itself a member of the political elite—contrasts itself with another mysterious element of "the establishment", i.e. a "deep state" that is "bullying" the party. The party has been openly hostile toward Russia, yet it recently hosted Marine Le Pen despite her many pro-Russian statements.

European elections in May 2019 where EKRE won 1 of the country's 7 seats confirmed its Euroscepticism. The party put forward the slogan "We protect Estonia's independence in Europe". It argued that EU institutions hold too much supranational power and that the bloc should focus on the economic aims of European integration like free trade and competitiveness while staying as simple, unregulated, and intergovernmental as possible. EKRE represents a line of Euro-populists which relies on polarization between the interests of the "EU elite" and Member States. In its political manifesto, it proposed several radical ideas regarding the EU. It suggested amending the Lisbon Treaty to make it less federal and more intergovernmental in order to protect the sovereignty of the member states. It demanded that EU members receive equal treatment, both in terms of representation in the European Parliament and in the bloc's agricultural payments. It additionally argued that Member States share similar values, such as protecting national sovereignty, should work together to enhance cooperation. Simultaneously, EKRE declared the EU should protect Christian culture and traditional European values, primarily by stopping immigration and deporting illegal immigrants. The party believes the EU should respect any nation's wish to join or leave the bloc, but it does not for the moment favour Estonia's withdrawal.

EKRE's success in the Estonian and European parliamentary elections in 2019 has given the party a platform to promote their ideas. EKRE now holds 19 seats from 101 seats in Estonia's parliament, this is up from 7 percent previously. Since the formation of Estonia's new government in April 2019, EKRE has been the dominant coalition partner, forcing its political agenda through mainly its skilful manipulation of the public opinion on the opinion of the government. This strong posture has created conflicts domestically and at the EU level.

EKRE's rhetoric is perplexing to many Estonians and has polarized Estonian society based on gender, race and educational level. Now, the focus is on growing differences within the Estonian community itself. Interestingly, Estonia's two main opposition parties, the Reform Party and the Social Democrats, contribute to the country's polarization, declaring that Estonia has turned away from European democratic values. However, it is worth noting that the same parties vocally supporting liberal values today played a major role in leading Estonia to its current political situation. Many Estonians are tired of being the EU's "poster child." They are stressed by socio-economic changes and feel left out from political debates. They are afraid of immigration, but behind it worry a lot about outmigration. This is why the EKRE party has provided a forum to express this frustration.

WHAT CAN BE DONE? SOME RECOMMENDATIONS

First, the liberal and social democratic opposition parties in Estonia, need to convince the population that it does not need to be protected from the state or the EU. To quote Estonia's slogan in its successful UN General Assembly campaign to become a non-permanent member of the UN Security Council: "Everyone has the right to respect and dignity." The same principle should apply to Estonia itself. Second, the EU representatives will need to demonstrate that European integration is not a project driven exclusively by the elite or benefiting just the centre. Third, Estonian mainstream or upcoming moderate parties need to seriously address some of the salient weaknesses of the hitherto dominant policies, especially the nearly unexisting regional policy in Estonia. But attention should also be given to the social policies that lay the burden of risk of losing normal livelihood, medical insurance with the loss of one's job Fourth, the EU should do attend to rethink its balance of monetary and fiscal policies. So far, only the ECB has played a significant role, but its monetary policy instruments are bound to remain severely restricted in alleviating the post-crisis problems in the Euro-area. Either the EU should introduce stronger fiscal lever, or it should change its policies with regard to deficit spending.

Finland: A Meaningful EU Debate Is Needed to Regain Ground from Populist Framing

Juha Jokela

The rise of the openly populist, Eurosceptic and right-leaning Finns Party has altered Finland's political landscape during the last ten years. It has led to the breakdown of national consensus on the country's pro-integrationist European Union (EU) policy. Recently, the Finns Party has moved further to the right and towards other European far-right parties, and focused on immigration and climate issues. Concurrently, the support ratings for the EU is at a record high in Finland. According to the recent Eurobarometers, 65 percent of Finnish people think that EU membership is a good thing, while 84 percent support the euro, and 70 percent would vote to remain in the EU. Relatedly, a new pro-European consensus on EU affairs is in the making among other political parties. These parties should not shy away from EU-related debates. On the contrary, they should aim to clarify their positions and, in doing so, clarify the differences among them. This is needed in order to regain ground from the populist framing of EU issues, which often aims at polarisation rather than a meaningful politicisation of EU affairs.

J. Jokela (✉)
Finish Insitute of International Affairs, Helsinki, Finland
e-mail: Juha.Jokela@fiia.fi

Towards Polarised EU Debates in Finland

Finland is often seen as the most integrationist of the Nordic EU Members States. In addition to the adoption of the single currency, the country has supported the transfer of competences to the EU level, strong EU institutions, qualified majority voting and a more unitary foreign and security policy. The country's integrationist policy path has been underpinned by a broad consensus among the political parties in EU affairs. Finnish EU policy makers have highlighted the benefits of constructive engagement in the EU. This has been seen to allow an accumulation of political capital, which could be used when significant national interests are at stake.

During the past ten years, severe European crises have re-energised the latent and partly marginalised Euroscepticism in Finland. The landslide victory of the Finns Party in the 2011 parliamentary election had notable ramifications for Finland's EU policy. Consequently, a more assertive Finnish EU policy emerged while the party was in the opposition in 2011–2015. Finland demanded collateral for the second Greek loan package and together with the Netherlands they blocked the entry of Bulgaria and Romania into the Schengen area.

The Finns Party's inclusion in the government after the 2015 election was seen to consolidate this turn, even if the party opted for more moderate EU positions to pave the way for a coalition government. While the government was argued to lack an EU vision and ambition, especially in the context of the Future of Europe debate propelled by Brexit, its EU posture was constructive rather than obstructive. It approved the third rescue loan package for Greece, which had previously been strongly opposed by the Finns Party. In the context of the migration crisis, Finland abstained from the vote to set up a temporary relocation system, but then became one of the few EU members to carry out agreed relocations. Moreover, the government's hesitance towards furthering the Economic and Monetary Union (EMU) reforms reflected a shared objective among the coalition partners.

The inclusion rather than exclusion of a challenger party has been seen as something typical of the Finnish political system and consensus tradition. The surge in Euroscepticism was geared towards a more moderate pathway, and governmental responsibilities including politically difficult decisions started to erode the support of the populist party. This strengthened the internal divisions in the Finns Party, and resulted in the party splitting in 2017. Half of the party's MPs formed a new group called the

Blue Reform and continued in the government, while the Finns Party moved into opposition and towards the populist far-right under new leadership.

The Finns Party's repositioning proved to be highly successful, and it managed to emerge as the second biggest party in the 2019 parliamentary election with 17.5 percent of support. While the election resulted in further fragmentation of the political landscape—none of the parties managed to gain 20 percent of the support—the populist Blue Reform collapsed and dropped out of parliament.

A Re-Emerging Pro-European Consensus, While Having a Strong Support for the Populist Alternative

The Finnish EU political landscape is currently characterised by two conflicting trends. On the one hand, a new national pro-European consensus on EU affairs seems to be emerging. It includes more or less all of the other parties in the current parliament, apart from the Finns Party. On the other hand, support for the Eurosceptic Finns Party is also increasing. Shortly after the 2019 election, it has assumed the lead in the polls with more than 20 percent backing.

Importantly, EU affairs were not among the central or most divisive issues in the 2019 election or in the ensuing coalition in government negotiations. Indeed, the lack of EU debate was one of the most striking features of the election, especially as it took place on the eve of the European Parliament elections and Finnish EU Council presidency.

The Finns Party largely focused on immigration and climate policy and did so from a domestic rather than an EU perspective. The party succeeded in providing a clear alternative to the other parties and in polarising the debate with their staunch criticism of immigration and alleged 'climate hysteria'.

However, this does not indicate that Euroscepticism is evaporating in Finland. Strong support for the Finns Party continues to have an impact on Finnish politics, with potential implications for Finnish EU policy. The party's more radical bearing has also been reflected at the EU level. After the 2019 EP elections, the party's two MEPs switched from the European Conservatives and Reformists (ECR) group to the far-right Identity & Democracy (ID) group in the European Parliament. The Finns Party did not manage to mobilise its supporters to the same extent as in the parliamentary election, however, and only secured 13.8 percent of the vote. The other 11 Finnish seats went to pro-European parties.

Nevertheless, with the notable exception of the Finns Party, recent national debates on EU affairs and to the extent that such debates have taken place have been rather consensual. Within a more turbulent security policy environment and in the context of increasing global economic and political competition, a stronger EU is clearly a broadly shared aspiration among Finland's parties.

What Can Be Done? Some Recommendations

There is a danger that the re-emerging domestic consensus on the EU, which is backed by increased public support for the EU in Finland, will lead to a closure of the national debate on EU affairs. This should be resisted, and the parties should seize the moment and approach the favourable political climate as an opportunity to open up the political space for informed national debates and decisions related to the character of the EU and the substance of its policies. This would enable the parties to better address some of the concerns channelled through the openly populist party such as immigration, economic prospects and social justice in an increasingly volatile regional and global environment.

Open debates among political parties on different policy options are indeed needed to regain ground from the populist framing of EU issues, which often aims at simplistic polarisation rather than a more meaningful politicisation of EU affairs. Such a debate would enable the parties and the electorate to weigh complicated issues related to future EU reforms and possible new crises.

The current political environment in Finland certainly invites the distinctively pro-European government to lay out a clear vision of the aspired development of the EU, as well as to define its position on the most important EU policies. These include Finland's position vis-à-vis further EMU reforms, the ambition to move towards a full-fledged 'defence union' by 2025, demands for more differentiated integration across a number of policy sectors, and the role of coalitions of Member States in EU decision-making. This includes the so-called 'New Hanseatic League' of eight northern EU members.

France: When Euroscepticism Becomes the Main Credo of the Opposition

Nonna Mayer and Olivier Rozenberg

Nine of the 39 lists competing for the 2019 European elections in France can be considered as Eurosceptic. If together they won 36 per cent of the vote, two of them would take the lion's share: the list of France Unbowed (LFI) led by Jean-Luc Mélenchon on the far left and the list of the National Rally (RN, formerly National Front) led by Marine Le Pen on the far right. Today the most dynamic of the two is by far the RN, whose leader qualified for the second round of the 2017 presidential election and whose lists finished top in the last two European elections, ending up with a score that was nearly four times higher than LFI's (23.3 per cent vs. 6.3 per cent) in 2019.

French Euroscepticism has ancient roots which strengthened at each step of the European integration process, giving birth to a new cleavage that cuts through the left-right divide. If we put aside the strong opposition of the Gaullists and the communists in the 1950s, the first appearance dates back to the 1992 referendum on the Maastricht Treaty, which was narrowly approved by 51 per cent of the French electorate. In spite of

---

N. Mayer • O. Rozenberg (✉)
Centre for European Studies and Comparative Politics of Sciences Po, Paris, France
e-mail: nonna.mayer@sciencespo.fr; olivier.rozenberg@sciencespo.fr

their internal divisions, the Treaty was supported by the centre-left (Socialist party) and centre-right parties (Union for French Democracy). It was however massively rejected by the extreme left and the extreme right and to a lesser degree by the Gaullist right (Rally for the Republic). 83 per cent of the communists, 93 per cent of the National Front supporters and 70 per cent of the Gaullists voted "No". The communists were against the Europe of big business and neoliberalism; the right and the far right saw it as a threat to national sovereignty and identity. But their profile was similar. The "No" mobilized the most disadvantaged voters, the working classes, in rural areas and small towns; the "Yes" won in big cities, among the richest and most educated voters. The same social and territorial cleavage reappeared at the time of the referendum on the Constitutional Treaty in 2005, which was rejected by 55 per cent of the voters, and in all European elections since.

In the 2010s, Euroscepticism gained ground in France. On the far left, Mélenchon, a former socialist, created a radical left movement and largely focused his discourse on criticizing the "ultraliberal" Europe. On the far right, Marine Le Pen, who inherited her father's party in 2011, vilified a "totalitarian" Europe, urging to make France "free again". Both leaders played with the idea of a "Frexit" without assuming it totally. The focus of the radical opposition discourse on the European Union (EU) worked well, as indicated by the National Rally's first position in the European elections of 2014 and 2019. This lasting success was fuelled by several major events throughout this period (the 2008 recession, the refugees' crisis, the wave of terrorist attacks). And Euroscepticism gave coherence to the policy discourses of the radical right by mixing traditional issues (protection against migration) and more recent ones (protection against social dumping).

The capacity of the European issue to restructure the party system was obvious in the 2017 presidential election. Together Mélenchon and Le Pen's parties drew 42 per cent of the votes in the first round, while the combined lists of the Socialist and Republican party garnered barely more than a quarter. The second round, for the first time in a national election, was dominated by the European cleavage, dramatically framed by Macron as the confrontation between progressives and nationalists, open and closed society, liberal vs. illiberal democracy and order vs. chaos. As in the Maastricht referendum, the defence of the EU mobilized the urban, well-off, educated elites while Le Pen appealed to the "forgotten", the working and the lower/middle classes.

Defeated, in spite of her record score of 34 per cent, Marine Le Pen slightly changed her strategy. She moderated her opposition to the euro currency, considering her radical anti-EU positions had been the main reason for her defeat, especially among elderly voters. As for many other nationalist parties in Europe, "Changing Europe from within" became her new motto. Today in France only small parties still defend Frexit, getting less than 2 per cent of the votes in the last European elections. But the opposition to President Macron is still largely focused on the criticism of his pro-EU credos, be it on the radical left or the radical right. The Yellow Vests movements that started in November 2018 brought confirmation that blaming the centrist President and the EU were closely connected issues. A survey we conducted just after the European elections (https://www.sciencespo.fr/centre-etudes-europeennes/node/26910) showed that the more a person agreed with the movement's claims, the higher were her scores on a scale of Euroscepticism, from 10 per cent among those who did not agree at all to 40 per cent if they agreed.

So far, though, the rise of Euroscepticism in French politics has had no major consequences on the European policy of French authorities. This is largely due to the strength of the French President within the domestic institutional system: Sarkozy (2007–2012) or Hollande (2012–2017) had the capacity to follow the agenda without compromising too much with the critical voices from their camp. There is also a remarkable continuity of the pro-EU commitment of French officials, including senior civil servants, that protected Brussels' day-to-day bargains from domestic politics. Yet, occasionally, French positions have moved. For instance, the reluctance of the socialist Prime Minister Manuel Valls (2014–2016) to welcome refugees can be understood as a consequence of the radical right rise. The French right is more critical vis-à-vis some aspects of the European integration, especially in the Schengen zone, compared to more than a decade ago.

What Can Be Done? Some Recommendations

Our recommendation regarding the Euroscepticism in France would be to integrate more of the left and right radical forces into the political game. Their discourse is largely fed by their quasi-exclusion from any parliamentary representation. With the two-round plurality voting system, the National Rally only won 1 per cent of the National Assembly seats in 2017 and Mélenchon's party 3 per cent, although they drew respectively 11 per cent and 13 per cent of the votes in the first round. A fairer representation of those groups would have then forced the government to justify and explain its European policy more frequently and more precisely—something which is only done now at elections time. The obligation made to the President to participate in the plenary debates (currently, legally forbidden) around European Councils would also feed the debates. In addition, the deficit of the French media coverage of Brussels' activities is a well-known phenomenon that should be fought against, in order to have a more accurate discussion depicting positions in favour of or against the EU. With a fairer voice for Eurosceptic views and more institutionalized and covered EU debates, the French public debate could address the very content of the European integration, going beyond the Manichean opposition between open and closed society. In addition, an opening of the party lists during the European elections could also be an incentive for incumbent MEPs to campaign.

Germany: Eurosceptics and the Illusion of an Alternative

Katrin Böttger and Funda Tekin

For decades Germany's European policy has been determined by parties, media and civil society that generally supports deeper European integration. In the early 1990s the first cracks materialized in this so-called 'permissive consensus': the Christian Social Union (CSU) repeatedly denounced a loss of national sovereignty; the Greens criticised regressive environmental policies and democratic deficits; and individual voices in the left party (Die Linke) declared the EU to be militaristic, neoliberal and undemocratic. However, it was the Alternative für Deutschland (AfD) that made hard Euroscepticism in Germany publicly respectable during the management of the financial crisis in the eurozone, which had started at the end of 2009. For some, the foundation of this right-wing to far-right political party in 2013 represents a liberation of political discourse in terms of finally being allowed to say what one thinks for others the alternative is nothing but an illusion and a dangerous one, too.

Apparently—and for most of us surprisingly—the AfD seems to be here to stay. At the last federal elections in 2017 for the first time in history this

---

K. Böttger (✉) • F. Tekin
Institut für Europäische Politik, Berlin, Germany
e-mail: Katrin.Boettger@iep-berlin.de; Funda.Tekin@iep-berlin.de

© The Author(s) 2021
M. Kaeding et al. (eds.), *Euroscepticism and the Future of Europe*,
https://doi.org/10.1007/978-3-030-41272-2_13

openly Eurosceptic party entered the German Bundestag and achieved representation at the national level. The AfD gained 91 seats and the third largest vote share after the Christian Democrats (CDU) and the Social Democrats (SPD). Consequently, building a coalition government was very difficult and ultimately led to another grand coalition. At the regional level, the AfD has been able to consolidate a much longer trend since 2014, when it first entered regional parliaments by even increasing its voter potential. Since 2018 the AfD is represented in all 16 state parliaments, with a much stronger base in the East German Lander with up to 27 percent in Saxony after the recent regional election of 1 September 2019.

There are three reasons why one gets accustomed to AfD's continued presence in German EU politics:

First, the AfD's trademark approach is the emotionalization of topics, underlining how everyone is supposedly affected by any given policy. At the time of its foundation, the party was a single-issue party opposing further European integration and was critical of the Euro and bailout of Greece and neither were part of the official government policy. However, the AfD managed to strongly influence the discourse on economic governance in Germany. With the ebbing of the economic and financial crisis, the AfD lost substantial grounds but with the large and partially undocumented influx of almost 900,000 refugees to Germany, a new crisis provided strong tailwinds in 2015. As a reaction, the AfD started to shift its focus towards anti-migration policies using it also as a reference point for its positions on other policy areas including the welfare state, security policy, and the current economy.

Second, the AfD's strategy is that of staged scandalization, influencing the public perception with "AfD topics". Both in the national and in the European elections the AfD had an above average media and social media coverage. For example, the protests in Chemnitz in 2018, that started after a Cuban German was killed by refugees, triggered the re-emergence of strong tensions regarding the issue of immigration to Germany, and served as a strong catalyst for AfD's policies. It is widely agreed that the party further radicalized in the course of these events and with this strategy the AfD was able to increase its representation in the European Parliament by four seats. In the end reaching 11 seats in 2019.

Third, the rise of the AfD has had effects on the national and regional governments' EU policies and political discourse. In indirect terms, this was most visible in the 180-degree turn of the government's rhetoric on its migration policy in 2018. The Federal Minister of Interior, Horst Seehofer (CSU), was strongly driven by the regional elections in Bavaria and the threat of losing votes to the AfD when he developed his 'masterplan for migration' that almost caused the break-up of the coalition government. Additionally, the fact that the AfD is represented in the Bundestag allows the party to directly impact policy-making through agenda-setting (e.g. interpellation in the Bundestag) or demands for committees of inquiry. Such as in the case of the attack on the Berlin Christmas market in 2016, after which the Bundestag signed off on security policy measures that would have been unthinkable even five or six years ago.

What Can Be Done? Some Recommendations

The rise of the AfD is a manifestation of a cleavage between cosmopolitical and nationalistic world views, the latter being convinced that the national level is better equipped to fend of negative effects of globalization. Considering the achievements of the European project, and with regard to the relative shrinking of European influence in the world, however, it is clear that despite existing weaknesses, there is no true alternative to European integration. Germany is comparably a newcomer in having to deal with hard forms of populist right-wing Euroscepticism that seem to be deeply rooted in society. Having to adapt to this situation without giving into the illusion of an alternative to the European integration project for the future of Europe.

One should be bolder and more proactive in communicating, explaining and supporting the integration project. This requires constructive presentation of reform proposals that acknowledge and clearly answer imperfections of the European integration project. The public and political discourse is required to walk the thin line between avoiding to provide a stage for and victimising populist Eurosceptic positions by shutting them out. Political parties are well advised to voice their own visions without trying to bandwagon on AfD-positions because this would not win them any votes.

Greece: The Remarkable Defeat of Euroscepticism

George Pagoulatos

Greece emerged from the July 2019 national elections with one of the most stable, pro-European Union (EU) and moderate party systems in the EU. This is remarkable given the depth, duration and debilitating socioeconomic legacy of the country's Great Recession. During 2008–2016 Greece lost a quarter of its GDP, unemployment peaked at 27 percent. Yet, following the elections of July 2019, four out of six parties represented in Parliament (entry threshold at 3 percent) are committed to Greece's participation in the European institutions and the euro: centre-right ND (158 seats), left-wing SYRIZA (86), socialist KINAL (formerly known as PASOK) (22), and left-wing MERA25 (9). All four of these parties (which add up to 275/300 seats) strongly support Greece's European vocation, though at least two of them (SYRIZA and MERA25) and have been highly critical of certain EU policies, especially regarding the eurozone.

Two remaining parties in Parliament carry a strongly Eurosceptic stance. The first is the orthodox communist party KKE (15 seats),

---

G. Pagoulatos (✉)
Hellenic Foundation for European and Foreign Policy (ELIAMEP), Athens, Greece

© The Author(s) 2021
M. Kaeding et al. (eds.), *Euroscepticism and the Future of Europe*,
https://doi.org/10.1007/978-3-030-41272-2_14

traditionally advocating Greece's exit from the EU and the euro. The second is a new ultra-right nationalist-populist party, Greek Solution (10), which owes its existence to the nationalist sentiment unleashed in Greek Macedonia against the recognition of the neighbouring Republic of North Macedonia under that name. Greek Solution succeeded the far-right Golden Dawn, which failed to enter Parliament, as well at the nationalist-populist Independent Greeks (ANEL). They are former coalition partners of SYRIZA in government and fell below the 3 percent bar. Like its predecessors, Greek Solution thrives on conspiracy theories and nationalistic, anti-EU, anti-Western and pro-Russia discourse, even though it does not explicitly promote an exit from the EU. So, the total presence of Eurosceptic parties in the Greek Parliament amounts to 25 out of 300 MPs.

This is a clear improvement from the previous Parliaments, where the anti-EU nationalistic vote was represented by the ultra-right Independent Greeks (ANEL) and the neo-Nazi Golden Dawn. In the June 2012 elections, Golden Dawn entered Parliament for the first time with 18 MPs, with ANEL gaining 20 seats; these were reduced to 18 and 10 respectively following the September 2015 general election. Most notably, between the elections of January and September 2015, and upon signing the country's 3rd bailout program, SYRIZA lost its more leftist, radical and communist-leaning faction, which was Eurosceptic and nationalistic. Then after September 2015, the party-political shift towards the pro-EU mainstream characterized both the left and the right on the parliament spectrum.

The July 2019, national election followed the European elections of May 2019. Typically, in the European elections, anti-EU parties tend to do better than in national elections. The European elections offer the opportunity of a protest vote, being perceived as midterm elections where stakes are lower. In the May EP elections, Golden Dawn obtained 4.9 percent of the vote (electing 2 MEPs), Greek Solution 4.2 percent (1 MEP), and several other parties fell below the 3 percent threshold. There is no doubt that the nationalist and Eurosceptic right is present in society, in a percentage area that ranges well above 10 percent and ends up voting for the largest right-of-centre party, the ND.

Three major issues over the last decade have created favourable conditions for nationalist and Eurosceptic stances. The economic crisis provided ample opportunity for blaming the EU for the harsh austerity after 2010, and was an opportunity grabbed by right populists. A left-wing populism spiced with harsh rhetoric against the EU status quo was employed by SYRIZA in its ascent from a small party of the radical left to the government in 2015. This rhetoric was swiftly abandoned following the 2015 referendum and 3rd bailout. Immigration was the second issue that gave ammunition to the far right, especially as irregular migration and refugee flows grew. Finally, the Prespa agreement with North Macedonia by the Tsipras government awakened nationalist sentiment in Northern Greece. The prompt opposition of ND to the Prespa agreement allowed it to claim the greatest part of the public opinion majority opposed to the compromise, thus sucking the oxygen of smaller nationalist far right parties.

The positive image emitted by parliamentary parties may misrepresent public opinion stances, which display great pessimism and diminished confidence in the EU, despite continuing majority support to EU membership and the euro. In Eurobarometer surveys, satisfaction with the EU conjures one of its lowest percentages in Greece, even though Greeks exhibit a higher than EU average percentage of support for more integration on every single EU policy area. So, in the first Eurobarometer survey following the EP elections, Greeks registered the 4th lowest score on whether their country has overall benefited from being an EU member. On the question does "my voice count in the EU" Greeks registered the 2nd lowest score in the survey. They had the 2nd highest percentage expressing disagreement as the main reason for voting in the recent EP elections. (Still, remarkably, the percentages of anti-EU parties remained low compared to the rest of the EU). Priority issues are unemployment, the economy and immigration, areas where Greeks believe they have not received sufficient EU support. Economy and growth received the highest percentage in Greece (and the highest compared to all other issue areas) as the key voting drivers in the EP elections.

Government policy has shown significant continuity across governments and parties, with the exception of the first Syriza-ANEL government during January–July 2015. Governments have been aligned with EU mainstream when it comes to support for deeper institutional and political integration, further enlargement towards the Western Balkans, and the completion of EMU. Greek governments under both Tsipras and currently Mitsotakis have been aligned to the EU policy on migration demanding EU support in better protecting external borders and burden-sharing across the EU. Despite being a main entry gateway of migrants and refugees through the Aegean, and hosting tens of thousands of refugees, Greek governments, including the current one, have overall refrained from adopting the anti-immigrant rhetoric identified with the likes of Salvini and Orban.

What Can Be Done? Some Recommendations

To deal with Euroscepticism Greece should substantially contribute to the ongoing dialogue on the Future of Europe. On a number of issues, future EU decisions and policies will be crucial for Greece. The Greek government and parties need to contribute their own input and coordinate action with other like-minded political actors in the EU. Issues of specific importance for Greece include: the fiscal, financial, economic and political integration of EMU, including a shift towards less fiscal austerity and greater support of investment; burden sharing on managing migration flows; progress towards common foreign and security policies and the defence union; energy and digital market union; implementation of the sustainability agenda towards carbon neutrality; the evolution of the common agricultural policy and structural and cohesion funds. A more active engagement for Greece on these and other issues of the Future of Europe agenda, at the levels of government, parties and civil society. This would include citizen participation, and would both strengthen a sense of European identity among Greek citizens and contain tendencies towards Euroscepticism.

Most importantly, Greece needs to address the main social drivers of Euroscepticism: joblessness, socioeconomic vulnerability and widespread insecurities that are morphing into not just anti-EU sentiment but anti-immigrant and xenophobic stances. Without a drastic decline of unemployment and a creation of better-paying jobs, such negative stances will persist. Without more effective policies of social integration of incoming immigrants and refugees, right-wing populists could see their electoral appeal increasing again over the years to come. Effective national governance and policies that deliver for the many are typically the best defence against anti-EU politics.

Hungary: Euroscepticism and Nationalism

András Inotai

Euroscepticism can be interpreted in two ways. It can refer to those parties (groups, NGOs and citizens) who would like to take back control from Brussels and enhance the manoeuvring room of national governments and decision-makers. Less power and competence in European Union (EU)-level organizations and broader "national sovereignty" of the member states. However, there is another interpretation as well. There are a number of EU-friendly parties (organizations and citizens) whose Euroscepticism stems from the inadequate and low-profile activities of EU-level organizations (partly limited by EU legislation and decisive competence of the European Council with extensive national veto rights) in a rapidly changing world, where the EU should become a global political and remain a global economic power.

Concerning the Hungarian party structure, there is practically no left-wing extremism or left-wing Euroscepticism. On the contrary, there have been substantial shifts on the right wing of the party structure. Jobbik (Better/Right), originally an anti-EU party, started to move towards the centre and has recognized the value added of the EU membership, even if criticizing "Brussels interference into domestic issues" in specific policy

---

A. Inotai (✉)
Institute of World Economics, Hungarian Academy of Sciences, Budapest, Hungary
e-mail: inotai.andras@krtk.mta.hu

areas. At the same time, the governing FIDESZ made a turn to the extreme right, mixing Euroscepticism with evident anti-EU attitude which opened an outdated but dangerous nationalistic rhetoric. FIDESZ, while Hungary's economic development (or even financial survival) is obviously linked to EU transfers (in per capita terms, Hungary is the largest beneficiary of the cohesion and structural funds amounting to almost 3 per cent of its annual GDP, but due to the uneven disbursement of EU money, in the last two years of the MFF, this sum may reach up to 4.5 to 5 per cent of GDP), is not only blaming Brussels for any interference into "national issues" (including the eventual and very loose control of how EU resources are spent). FIDESZ, from the very beginning in 2010, has been violating basic European values (from democracy through media freedom to rule of law). In addition, it has blocked several EU resolutions (from environment to Africa and Ukraine). Moreover, it implemented an election campaign against the EU as the main enemy of migration (the posters with Soros and Juncker have disappeared but "decorated" the streets over months). It invited (and supported by HUF 3.1 bn) a rather suspicious "international" bank established in Russia to move its headquarters to Budapest. Viktor Orbán's special relation to Vladimir Putin is well-known and mainly serves the undermining of the European integration from within the EU. (Let alone his ties and commitments to China, Turkey, Central Asia, Arab contacts, all of them not in line with key European security and political priorities.) For the most recent and absolutely shameful actions, see Orbán's visit to the Turk Council event held in Baku in October 2019 and meeting with Erdogan a few days after Turkey attacked Syria or Erdogan's official visit to Hungary in November 2019. And there is no EU-level response.

In the last national elections, FIDESZ, for the third time, obtained a two-thirds majority in the Hungarian Parliament, with 30 per cent of the votes of the population and fewer votes than the dis-united opposition together (31 per cent). The success is due to the highly distorted (undemocratic) election system which started to be "reformed" in 2011 and the overwhelming domination of media, particularly outside Budapest and some major regional centres. The successful and (up to today) unstoppable campaign against any kind of migration, has created a widespread mental contamination in a large part of the Hungarian society, and is one of the major in-built bottlenecks against relevant change to more EU-friendly attitude in the foreseeable future. Despite the fundamental democratic deficit, FIDESZ managed to increase the number of MEPs in the last European Parliament (EP) elections by 1 seat (from 12 to 13), although the Prime Minister expected up to 16 representatives out of 21 Hungarian EP members. Out of 21 EP seats for Hungary, 13 went to FIDESZ, 4 to the Democratic Coalition, 2 to Momentum and 1 each to MSZP (socialists) and to Jobbik (Right). The rapid rise of two EU-friendly parties, Democratic Coalition and Momentum, can be attributed to their clear pro-EU position and the mobilization of a substantial part of the society. In fact, and despite all anti-EU propaganda of the government, the Hungarian society still belongs to those among EU member countries where the EU is considered a positive factor supported by 70 per cent of the population.

The Eurosceptic and anti-EU government did not change its EU-related policy, just the opposite. Its two-thirds majority in the national elections was interpreted (and misused) as a mass supporter to the anti-EU attitude of the government (concerning migration, against Brussels interference into domestic issues and the uncontrolled use of EU resources).

The obvious but officially not admitted backlash in the outcome of the 2019 EP elections destroyed Orbán's calculation about a strong right-wing and anti-EU party. With suspended membership in the European People's Party (EPP) group, he had firm hopes for a strong Eurosceptic to anti-EU party alliance in the new EP. The gain of one additional seat in the EP did not convince the European People's Party to open up to Orbán's faithful partners, such as the ÖVP or Salvini, and move the EPP further to the "illiberal" right position. Although there has been a basic difference between Orbán and Salvini concerning migration. While both would prohibit illegal migration, Salvini's other priority was to redistribute migrants among EU member countries, which met fierce opposition from Orbán.

In order to push the defeat and its potential consequences into the background, the Hungarian government started a new counterattack in various fields: (a) intensifying communication against any kind of EU-level migration agreement; (b) strengthening Hungary's bulwark position in defending "Christianity" (Orbán redefined Hungary as "Christian democracy", instead of an (il)liberal one); (c) strongly opposing Hungary's joining of the EU Prosecutor Office, including any meaningful OLAF control of misusing EU resources; (d) reinterpreting the EU environmental rules in the United Nations (UN) environment conference by János Áder, the President of Hungary, and, allegedly, a prominent fighter for climate protection; (e) defending the potential EU Commissioner from Hungary against (just and rightful) attacks in the shaping of the Ursula von der Leyen Commission; (f) and last but not least, organizing provocative personal meetings with anti-EU (far-right) parties. The latest examples are his meeting with Norbert Hofer, the successor of Strache representing the far-right Austrian party and his various visits to Italy, including a speech at the post-fascist party conference of the Fratelli d'Italia and his obvious turn to Turkey and Central Asia.

Preparing for municipal elections (in October 2019), the government is generating additional anti-EU sentiments by brand marking all opposition parties as supporters of opening up the Hungarian borders to migrants. Despite a massive predominance of the information channels, the municipal elections resulted in a clear victory of the opposition and the hardly digestible defeat of FIDESZ. Budapest and ten other major towns became governed by the united opposition. Although FIDESZ could keep its majority in the province, the historically developed dividing line between the globally opened metropolitan areas (social strata) and the short-minded nationalist provincial areas has been strengthened. Under these circumstances, it would not be striking if the ruling party's ideological campaign continued with enhanced intensity and evident anti-democratic and anti-EU character. Despite the intensive work of the Finnish EU Presidency, the infringement procedure is unlikely to make any meaningful progress, let alone to affect the government's basic policy line.

What Can Be Done? Some Recommendations

In Hungary, there needs to be a strong coalition of opposition parties that should not be broken down after the success achieved in the municipal elections. Further cooperation is needed in order to limit the government's antidemocratic and anti-EU activities (including money, media dominance and mental contamination of large parts of the society). Furthermore, there needs to be a constant dialogue with pro-EU groups and institutions (70 per cent of the population considers itself an indisputable winner of EU membership, due to free trade, EU money, Schengen and the free movement of people and workers). However, there remains a democratic deficit due to 600,000 Hungarians, overwhelmingly in favour of deepening ties with the EU, not being able to vote due to the restrictive rules applied to Hungarian citizens living and working in another EU member country.

On the EU level, the EU's scope of activity definitely depends on what kind of EU will emerge: a new global power with fundamental deepening or a loose EU with clear tendencies of disintegration. Only in the case of a fundamental deepening the following recommendations are valid:

1. The EU and key member countries have a historical responsibility in not having stopped the undemocratic and anti-EU politics of the Hungarian government just after 2010, when basic values and the rule of law were clearly neglected. This was without any reaction, therefore, providing further fuel to undermining the EU's legal and institutional structure.
2. Immediate and strong control of the misuse of EU resources, including the stopping of further financing and reclaiming misused and abused money.
3. In the framework of the ongoing negotiations on the MFF 2021–2027, clear linking of the transfer of money to the observation of basic European values and rule of law and the permanent and direct control of using EU funds.
4. Immediate investigation of the status (and goals) of the Russian International Investment Bank in Budapest.
5. Following the setback of Trócsányi, as the only potential EU commissioner of Hungary unequivocally supported by Orbán, a new candidate appeared (the current head of the Permanent Representation of Hungary in Brussels), but Ursula von der Leyen demanded a second woman candidate as well, without any response by Orbán. However, the key issue is not the person but the portfolio. Any Hungarian would-be commissioner for the position of "enlargement and neighbourhood policy" has to be immediately blocked for two reasons. First, a country (better to say, his PM) that has smuggled out of Macedonia a former Prime Minister who had been sentenced to jail and provided him asylum in Hungary (Gruevski, as a close friend of Viktor Orbán) cannot be entitled as responsible for the Western Balkans, which includes North Macedonia. Second, Hungary, based on short-sighted interests and anti-EU propaganda, has blocked the EU's comprehensive approach to Ukraine. A country blocking the EU's neighbourhood policy is definitely not only unsuitable to represent the EU but would be obviously discrediting and destroying any EU-level neighbourhood approach.

6. Convince the EPP that, taking into account Orbán's consequent undermining of the EU and his most recent shameful and deliberately provocative steps, FIDESZ should be immediately excluded from the party family. If it does not happen, the EU itself is eliminating its creditworthiness.
7. All transnational companies working in Hungary (not least the German ones), at least within the EU, have not only had corporate social responsibility (CSR) but also corporate political responsibility. They should disregard short-term economic interests and should not cooperate with a government undermining the EU.
8. Enhanced communication on all levels, including EU-friendly Hungarian parties, institutions, NGOs and civic fora in cooperation with Hungarian partners.

Most importantly the EU should (a) present and communicate the future of the EU as a strong global political and economic entity prepared to successfully manage global challenges; (b) provide substantial deepening in various areas, more community-level competence and meaningful limitation of national veto rights; (c) have a strict control of the use of EU resources and clear and immediate consequences of any breach of European values and rules of law; and (d) get prepared for being able to manage a two (or more)-speed Europe by leaving the door open for member countries reluctant to join selected EU policies at the moment but not taking any responsibility for the potential consequences of self-marginalization and self-peripheralization.

Iceland: Hard-Line Eurosceptics Clash with Eurosceptics

Baldur Thorhallsson

Most political parties represented in the Althingi, the Icelandic national parliament, are Eurosceptic in the sense that they oppose Iceland's membership in the European Union (EU). Nevertheless, the vast majority of them support Iceland's membership in the European Economic Area (EEA) and Schengen, and there is a cross party consensus on membership in the European Free Trade Association (EFTA). However, in recent years, the Icelandic political party system has become increasingly polarized around European integration. New Eurosceptical and pro-European parties have emerged, which either campaign to limit Iceland's participation in the EEA and Schengen, or to join the EU. The established political parties which prefer the status quo have joined forces in a cross right-left coalition government. They have had to fight off fierce opposition from the Eurosceptic hard-liners to the implementation of the Third Energy Package of the EU within the EEA framework and pressure from the Europhiles to re-open the accession talks with the EU.

In the last decade, following Iceland's economic collapse in 2008, the party system has become more fragmented and the traditional four party

---

B. Thorhallsson (✉)
Insitute of International Affairs, University of Iceland, Reykjavík, Iceland
e-mail: baldurt@hi.is

system (occasionally with the fifth party presented in the Althingi) has become a multi-party system. In the last general election in 2017, eight political parties gained a seat in the Althingi and the elections saw the rise of the two new Eurosceptic populist parties, the Centre Party and the People's Party. They have increasingly sought to oppose the implementation of EEA acts and criticize Iceland's membership in Schengen, especially with regards to border control and associated policies towards migrants and asylum seekers. The parties ran a vigorous campaign against the implementation of the Third Energy Package in 2019, adopting a nationalist discourse in their campaign—a typical political discourse in Iceland, which has shaped all European debates in the past. Their main claim was that the new acts would transfer sovereignty from Iceland to the EU institutions. This claim has been an ongoing theme in the European debate in Iceland, and using it was an easy task in the aftermath of the intensive debate about Iceland's accession talks with the EU in 2009–2013.

The Centre Party was formed by the former Prime Minister and leader of the centre-agrarian Progressive Party, Sigmundur Davíð Gunnlaugsson, only a month before the 2017 general elections. The party advocates strong adversary politics and has clear populist overtones. Gunnlaugsson, a former well-known TV reporter, became a celebrated figure in Icelandic politics because of his strong opposition to the so-called Icesave deal between the government of Iceland and the governments of Britain and the Netherlands. He portrayed Icelanders who advocated for the deal as traitors to Iceland's sovereignty and independence, and harshly criticised the EU for allying itself with its Member States and not standing by Iceland within the EEA framework. In the 2017 elections, the Centre Party obtained 11 percent of the votes and had seven MPs elected. At present, the parliamentary group of the Centre Party has nine members, after two out of four elected members of the People's Party joined it.

In 2017, the People's Party obtained 7 percent of votes after having failed to reach the 5 percent threshold to secure seats in the general election to Althingi a year earlier. The party also has a charismatic leader, Inga Sæland, who has become an advocate of increased public support to disabled people and pensioners, while also calling for the elimination of poverty in Iceland. The party's rhetoric clearly strikes a populist tone.

The Icelandic traditional four party system has always been dominated by the centre right Independence Party. The Conservatives have always hesitated to participate in the European project unless such a move is seen as necessary to deal with a crisis situation and they have only made such steps when the interests of the primary sectors have been firmly secured in any arrangements. Historically, the second largest party, the Progressive Party, has usually opposed closer engagement with European integration. The socialist party, now labelled the Left Green Movement, vigorously opposed all moves towards Europe, membership in the EFTA, the EEA and Schengen. However, the Left Greens have become more mainstream with regards to Iceland's present European policy. The smallest of the four parties, the Social Democratic Party (SDP), was the driving force behind membership in EFTA, and the EEA, and managed on both occasions to get its coalition member in government, the Independence Party, to support its European initiatives. The Social Democrats also initiated Iceland's EU membership application in 2009, just nine months after the economic crash, and its European policy prevailed in its coalition government with the Left Greens, up to the parties' devastating defeats in the elections in 2013 – after which a new coalition government consisting of the Independence Party and the Progressive Party put the EU membership application on hold.

At present, following the elections in 2017, the Independence Party, the Progressive Party and the Left Green Movement, form a governmental coalition. The government is firmly behind Iceland's engagement with the European project. In the past, the parties, while in government, have always stood by Iceland's concurrent engagement in Europe. Their opposition to participation in European integration while in opposition in the Althingi has undoubtedly populistic overtones. Nevertheless, the Independence Party was deeply divided on the implementation of the Third Energy Package. The current government opposes membership in the EU but has no intention to formally withdraw Iceland's EU membership application. The parties in government, as before, prefer the status quo.

To summarize, one could say that the three political parties in the coalition government joined forces in order to fight off the challenge from more liberal parties (the pro-European Reform Party, the Pirates, and the Social Democrats) in 2017. The liberal parties advocate structural changes of the Icelandic society, such as a new constitution, altered fisheries management system and membership in the European Union. Currently, the coalition members do face a rougher challenge from the two new populist parties, the Centre Party and the People's Party, which have adopted a nationalistic anti-European rhetoric.

What Can Be Done? Some Recommendations

Firstly, those who support Iceland's current engagement with the European project cannot sit on the side-lines any longer if they want to preserve this status. They have to speak up and convince voters that there are more benefits than costs associated with membership in the EEA and Schengen.

Secondly, the pro-European parties are in danger of losing the platform to the hard-line Eurosceptic parties if they do not step up their campaign for membership in the EU. The debate is increasingly centred around the status quo or more restricted participation in the EEA and Schengen.

Thirdly, the Icelandic Europhiles need to explain to voters the main difference between membership in the EEA and Schengen on the one hand, and membership in the EU on the other. For instance, they need to spell out what Iceland is missing out by not being a member of the EU's Structural Funds and that Iceland would have a say on EU/EEA legislation as a member of the Union.

Fourthly, if the EU and its Member States are serious about strengthening the Union and get robust democratic states to join them, they could take the initiative and offer Iceland (and Norway and Greenland) a special deal on fisheries and agriculture. An offer where Iceland's concerns about its primary sectors would be taken into account could trigger a new debate about Iceland's EU membership application.

Ireland: 'A Rising Tide Lifts All Boats'—A Unique Situation on Countering Euroscepticism

Róisín Smith

Ireland has quite a unique relationship with the European Union (EU). In the last ten years, Ireland has had to withstand harsh austerity policies, an economic recession, and an EU-International Monetary Fund (IMF) bailout, in which the EU was seen by some to be imposing stringent banking and financial regulation. Emigration and social inequality increased, and Ireland's national debt escalated. Yet, anomalously, Ireland remains consistently pro-European. Irish support for the EU is at its highest level in decades, with over ninety percent approval rating. How can this phenomenon be interpreted in the Irish context and why is this peculiar to Ireland?

While the EU has experienced a multitude of crises, which have played a major part in the creation of new populist and Eurosceptic parties across Europe, Ireland has not witnessed the manifestation of this political ideology. There are no true Eurosceptic parties influencing the political system. In many respects, Ireland is atypical. It represents a country on the periphery in more ways than one: an odd one out in the EU in terms of

R. Smith (✉)
Institute of International and European Affairs, Dublin, Ireland
e-mail: roisin.smith@iiea.com

© The Author(s) 2021
M. Kaeding et al. (eds.), *Euroscepticism and the Future of Europe*,
https://doi.org/10.1007/978-3-030-41272-2_17

Euroscepticism, and a resilient island at the furthest corner of Europe. This is not to suggest that attitudinal dimensions of populism and Euroscepticism do not exist in Ireland. Rather, there are no real discernible patterns to evidence that Euroscepticism or extreme nationalism are shaping the political landscape. An examination of political fragmentation and discontent, Ireland's geographical frontier in Europe, and the Brexit factor demonstrate that any measure of dissent in the political system is both local, distinctive and entirely dependent on context. Moreover, Ireland has been remarkably strong in promoting the values and benefits of EU membership.

POLITICAL FRAGMENTATION AND DISCONTENT

The economic turmoil that Ireland experienced from 2008 onwards, and the subsequent austerity policies initiated by the Irish government caused the fragmentation of the party system. It resulted in the dominant and centrist political party, Fianna Fáil, losing power in the 2011 general election. At that time, many incumbent parties in Europe were being voted out of office, punished for implementing harsh policies and adding to the rise in unemployment and inequality. These factors contributed to the rise of Euroscepticism and populist parties.

Levels of Euroscepticism exist in every EU Member State. In Ireland, there are varying degrees of anti-European, anti-establishment, anti-immigration and populist sentiments. Protest voting, political discontent and distrust for the governing parties did result in an increase in the vote for self-described 'Euro-critical' parties such as Sinn Féin, and gains for new groupings, for instance, the Anti-Austerity Alliance, People Before Profit and Independents in the 2016 general election. Notwithstanding this, it is inaccurate to overestimate and conflate the importance of anti-establishment and anti-elitist sentiment in the Irish context and in shaping the Irish voter towards an anti-European view. Anti-establishment sentiment, however, does not lead to a distinctly Eurosceptic force. Far from being decisively Eurosceptic, left wing parties in Ireland campaign to change the domestic status quo. Furthermore, Ireland's initial rejection of both EU treaties, Nice and Lisbon in their first referenda, had more to do with domestic and anti-establishment stances than hard Euroscepticism. This sentiment must be understood as local and contextual, idiosyncratic in determining the national debate, but not substantially anti-European.

Ireland is also a multi-party European democracy and uses proportional representation, single transferable vote (PR-STV). It does not have a radical right party. Due to the presence of PR-STV, the more traditional long-standing parties, like Fianna Fail and Fine Gael had strong affiliation with and loyalty to their party membership. This is evident in the ease with which a voter can access their local representative, an important factor in Ireland. Although there is far less allegiance to traditional parties nowadays, Irish voters discontented with the system can still express their voice and concerns directly to those in power.

Geographical Frontiers Matter

Ireland's geographical position on the periphery of the EU is also noteworthy. As a small nation next to a much larger neighbour in the UK, Ireland needed a broader economic perspective in which to grow separately as a nation. Ireland has deep historical links with the European continent and Ireland displayed an openness to EEC membership and a determination to be at the core of the European project from the start. Essentially, Ireland embraced a rising tide that would modernise and transform a largely rural and agricultural-based economy into a well-diversified economy, and a globally oriented and prosperous nation, on a per-capita basis. Irish people are acutely aware of the benefits of EU structural and cohesion funds, the socio-economic advantages of the EU's Social Policy and the EU's Common Agricultural Policy, all of which contribute to an overall pro-European outlook.

As an island nation, Ireland has not experienced massive flows of migration that other EU Member States have witnessed in recent years. For the most part, and throughout the 2000s, economic immigrants, from Eastern European states, in particular, have been welcomed into the Irish workforce. Asylum seekers also have a right to protection and integration, and Ireland has been generally positive about EU integration and EU enlargement.

The Brexit Factor

The UK vote in 2016 to leave the European Union has profound significance for Ireland. The unintended consequences of this monumental decision cannot be underestimated. The current Brexit conundrum is at odds with the close relationship the British and Irish governments had formed in recent decades, especially during negotiations for the Good Friday Agreement in 1998 and beyond. While the close relationship with the UK has been temporarily altered, the relationship with the EU has been greatly augmented. The unanimous solidarity the EU displayed towards Ireland, in light of the Brexit negotiations, has considerably enhanced the EU's standing in Ireland. The support of the other EU Member States has been deeply appreciated by the Irish.

Some had feared that the UK's withdrawal would trigger a domino effect, leading to the eventual demise of the European project. Quite the opposite has occurred in Ireland, where a putative 'Irexit' failed to find popular support. Instead of unhinging Europe, Brexit has harnessed support for the EU. The EU has spoken with one voice on Brexit not only in the interests of defending the Single Market, but also in defending the Irish peace process. Latest polls conducted in the summer of 2019 state that a high proportion of Irish people say that Brexit has improved their already favourable opinion of the EU.

What Can Be Done? Some Recommendations

In conclusion, Ireland grasped a rising tide that would lift all boats when it came to EU membership. In most sectors of Irish society, from the economic to the social to the educational sphere, the values and benefits of EU membership are clearly visible. Ireland has fully participated in EU decision-making and Ireland's adherence to European values of peace, democracy and the rule of law, have certainty contributed to a pro-European position. The EU will need to do more in Member States to further promote the incentives of membership, while reflecting and responding to citizen's concerns. Although Ireland has not escaped dimensions of Euroscepticism, the advantages of EU membership far outweigh any anti-European view. As such, Ireland's position can be viewed as unique in the discourse of Euroscepticism.

Italy: Has Salvini Saved the Country from Himself? Not Yet

Eleonora Poli

Since early September 2019, Italy is no longer led by a Eurosceptic government. The new yellow–red coalition composed of the Five Star Movement (M5S) and the Democratic Party (PD) was formed under a declared discontinuity with respect to the previous M5S–Lega government (yellow–green) on European issues. Ironically, such an outcome was actually caused by former Minister of Interior, Matteo Salvini, one of the most Eurosceptic political figures in Italy and in the European Union (EU), the leader of the Lega and founder of the Identity and Democracy group in the European Parliament.

In August 2019, Salvini presented a motion of no confidence against the Italian Prime Minister Giuseppe Conte. In his calculation this should have triggered a snap election that, according to the polls, he could have easily won. Yet, Salvini miscalculated that Italy is a parliamentary republic. If there is a political majority within the parliament, able to provide confidence in a new government within the five-year legislature term, there is no need for a new vote.

E. Poli (✉)
Istituto Affari Internazionali, Roma, Italy
e-mail: e.poli@iai.it

© The Author(s) 2021
M. Kaeding et al. (eds.), *Euroscepticism and the Future of Europe*,
https://doi.org/10.1007/978-3-030-41272-2_18

Salvini's hazardous political move did not come without cost. In less than a month, from being the Minister of Interior and one of the most powerful political figures in Italy, Salvini lost some consensus and became a simple Senator. Yet, he is still the leader of the first opposition party, with a popular support of around 32 percent registered in October 2019. Salvini justified his political miscalculation by accusing, among others, the EU and some Member States of conspiring against him. In his view, the yellow–red government and its whole cabinet were decided in Paris and in Berlin against the will of the Italians. He is right about one point, if the government is no longer Eurosceptic, Italian citizens' disenchantment towards the EU has not disappeared. If elections had been called in August 2019, chances of a pro-European government would have been very low.

While craving for national independence and nostalgia for a mythologised past are unfortunately a global trend, Euroscepticism in Italy was specifically favoured by the economic and social crises affecting the country since 2008. More than ten years after the outbreak of the global financial crisis, the growth of the Italian GDP is estimated at a modest 0.9 percent while unemployment is still around 10 percent Against this backdrop, since 2013 uncontrolled migration waves have been affecting mostly the unprivileged social classes, the same ones already hit by the economic downturn. This has contributed to spreading a sense of general insecurity and has fuelled nationalism.

By labelling the EU and the so-called "pro-European" traditional parties as incapable or unwilling to face the above issues, both the M5S and the Lega amplified Italian Euroscepticism. However, while being equally anti-EU and anti-euro, the two parties' respective campaigns for the March 2018 national elections focused on different types of voters. Beyond Euroscepticism, the M5S was all about the need to stop rising poverty through the fight against corruption, the introduction of a basic income scheme and the reduction of the privileges of the political caste both in Italy and in the EU. Support for the M5S came mostly from the South of Italy, where poverty and corruption are the main social plague. Differently, by claiming to be the unique party able to go against the will of Brussels and fight against insecurity, stop migration, cut taxes and reduce the retirement age, Lega gathered the most votes in the wealthier Northern regions, where citizens feared to lose their social and economic wellbeing.

It was only after entering into coalition with the M5S that the Lega gathered momentum, turning into the foremost party in Italy. This was because Salvini kept campaigning, even after being appointed Minister of Interior. The Salvini Tour, organised in the summer of 2019, was a series of events on Italian beaches calculated to spread an even more vivid nationalist and anti-European rhetoric. Indeed, having performed exceptionally in the May 2019 European elections (34 percent of the vote against 23 percent registered by the PD and 17 percent by the M5S) Salvini was convinced his party should have gained more power within the European institutions. This was not the case. Not only was Ursula Von der Leyen nominated President of the Commission against his will, but he was not able to appoint a Commissioner, and David Sassoli, a member of the centre-left PD, became the President of the European Parliament.

Differently from Lega, since the formation of the yellow–green government, the M5S has become more institutionalised, abandoning much of its anti-European rhetoric such as the idea of a referendum for exiting the eurozone. Although the party granted Salvini the political support needed to implement pension and security reforms, strongly criticised by the European institutions, and to close Italian ports to incoming migrants, it became less vocally Eurosceptic than Lega. Considering the support granted to the new Commission President as well as its attempt to enter a pro-European group in the aftermath of the EP elections, the M5S can no longer be considered openly anti-European. Granted, such a wind of change is not everlasting. As its last political switch demonstrates, having no ideology of reference or a precise political identity, the M5S is capable of changing political stance more easily than traditional parties do.

To date, only one Italian out of two is happy about the new government. Apparently, most Italians were against the political crisis caused by Salvini but feel betrayed by the yellow–red government, that was established without a popular vote. Chances are that, in the long run, the M5S–PD coalition could fuel anti-European sentiments even further if the socio-economic trends do not improve. Moreover, considering the fluidity of the Italian electorate, being in the opposition could allow Salvini to expand his popularity. Yet, the government-declared pro-EU shift, the appointment of former Prime Minister Gentiloni as Commissioner for the Economy, as well as the replacement of anti-euro Minister of European Affairs, Paolo Savona, could restore Italian political and economic credibility, resulting in the EU loosening some rigidities on economic and migration issues to the benefit of Italian citizens.

What Can Be Done? Some Recommendations

To restore faith in the EU, the yellow–red government needs to address Italy's burning issues at the European level. It takes better relations with France and Germany, which deteriorated during the yellow–green government, when Italy attempted to build closer ties with the Visegrad countries. Moreover, considering Brexit and the consequent reshuffling of Member States' relationships, Italy should go beyond the usual suspects and engage other key players, such as the Netherlands among others, to promote effective multilevel actions and improve socio-economic trends. This means, for instance, a new "solidarity pact", besides the Malta Agreement, to equally share the burden of the migration flows as well as support for economic actions such as a European Green Deal to respectively promote innovation and sustainable growth. Probably, it will take more than one legislature to restore trust in the EU. Yet, the only way this government could set the path towards real change is by being in the frontline when it comes to encouraging European policies that could benefit the country, leaving the Eurosceptic forces and Salvini as mere spectators.

Kosovo: Moonwalking Towards the European Union

Venera Hajrullahu

Kosovo's Unconditional EU-Love

True to its tradition, Kosovo remains a sui generis case even when it comes to Euroscepticism, which has been a trend that has flourished in the region and beyond. The young republic is undoubtedly the most pro-EU country in Europe, with many polls continuously showing well over 90 percent of public support for Kosovo's European Union (EU) integration. No wonder that the promise of an EU future has been a permanent fixture in most political parties' programs, but the question is not 'if', it's 'who can get there faster'.

For decades, every candidate across the political spectrum campaigned on being the right person to lead Kosovo towards its European dream. In other countries, populism is now intertwined with anti-EU sentiments, but for Kosovo, the EU was the populist choice. EU integration was seen as a process to benefit the whole society. It represents freedom and equality for all, and a chance to belong to a large family of progressive values. The

---

V. Hajrullahu (✉)
Change Experts Group, Pristina, Kosovo
e-mail: venera.hajrullahu@change-ks.com

© The Author(s) 2021
M. Kaeding et al. (eds.), *Euroscepticism and the Future of Europe*,
https://doi.org/10.1007/978-3-030-41272-2_19

nation breathed a collective sigh of relief when the Stability and Association Agreement (SAA) was signed in 2015. The EU was happening for Kosovo. The next step would finally be the long-coveted EU visa liberalization for Kosovo; unrelated to integration, but integral to the people.

Having suffered brutal oppression and denial of basic human rights for far too long, even a simple freedom such as being able to travel to the EU unhindered had become a goal in itself, rather than a means to ends. Long lines in front of EU embassies and intense screening procedures were becoming too reminiscent of a time when Kosovars felt that they were second-rate citizens.

Alas, a Love Unrequited

In 2015, the first crack down in Kosovo's unwavering EU support became apparent. As a condition for visa liberalization, the EU had asked Kosovo to pass the law on border demarcation with Montenegro, which two major opposition parties were staunchly against and perceived the proposed agreement as a loss of territory for Kosovo. It was the first time that MPs were asking out loud "is the EU worth it?". After a long stalemate on this critical issue, the parliament was dissolved in hopes that it was best to leave the decision to the people who would be heading to the voting polls. Popular support for the EU won again, and the contentious law was passed in 2016. In hopes that the EU would surely hold up their end now.

The carrot that the EU held over Kosovo's political parties and the people was never delivered. The Commission had given a positive recommendation, but it could not deliver on the visa liberalization decision. People familiar with the decision process would say that it was not their promise to make in the first place, but the overwhelming majority of Kosovars felt cheated. Not by Kosovo political parties, but by the European Union, as it was their own high officials that stood in front of the people and publicly promised visa free travel as soon as the demarcation law was passed.

And while Kosovo still does not have Eurosceptic parties per se, the once isolated, errant voices of Euroscepticism were heard sporadically and now have access across the entire political spectrum. This then turned into groups of people starting to ask how many more times the EU will bait into disregarding national interests in favour of empty promises. It is not even a matter of pointing the finger or shifting the blame for internal shortcomings in a country with over 90 percent of the popular support for the EU. If that support starts dwindling, there is only one logical address to hold accountable.

Too Little, Too Late?

This newly born pessimism in Kosovo was only further exacerbated by the diminishing perspective of EU integration for the Western Balkans. The European elections were watched closely with hopes that the EU accession prospect would regain some of its credibility, after being fraught with tensions and discord. Unfortunately, EU enlargement seems a distant possibility.

Kosovo remains the last country in Europe without EU visa liberalization. Just a few months after the 2019 European elections, Kosovo held its national elections and for the first time in a decade, EU visa liberalization was not among electoral promises by any party. For ordinary citizens the EU is becoming less attractive by the day and if political parties cannot bank on this perspective, they will surely move in favour of other options.

For Vetëvendosje, the left-wing party that won the elections for the first time, EU integration is much lower on the list of priorities compared to other parties in power until now. Following the EU's unsuccessful attempt to negotiate a final normalization of relations agreement between Kosovo and Serbia, due to a lack of coherent and consistent foreign policy, other major parties are now considering taking a more careful approach to negotiating with the EU.

What Can Be Done? Some Recommendations

The interpretation of a withdrawal from the EU integration perspective to the Western Balkans, and the EU's stance now seems to be that they are halting enlargement in order to prevent more growth of Euroscepticism. Meaning that the Western Balkans are not only unwelcome, but they pose a danger to the very fabric of the European Union. This has led to some countries in the region turning elsewhere for support and that elsewhere is anti-EU. This begs the question that is it more dangerous to have Euroscepticism within the EU, where it can have a chance of being contained? Or to have it on its borders, where countries feel that they are left out in the open to all sorts of radicalizations?

In what was called a historical mistake, France's veto to the opening of accession negotiations with Albania and North Macedonia is seen as a death sentence to the EU enlargement in general. The disenchantment and confusion this decision has provoked now call for a self-examination and repositioning of the region towards the EU. In doing so, Western Balkans countries would have the chance to turn themselves into actors that contribute to the shaping of the EU's enlargement policy. Kosovo should be part of this common effort while gradually reversing externally driven reform into an internally driven development agenda, owned by its political leadership and the society as a whole.

Latvia: Euroscepticism—Between Reason and Treason

Karlis Bukovskis and Andris Spruds

The scenery of Latvia's political parties does not differ much from the country's landscape in Autumn. Filled with political positions of various colours, kinds and shades, Latvian political parties struggle for a presence in the national parliament. Modern Latvia has not seen the classical left-right divisions that are characteristic of its Western-European counterparts and instead, has political cleavages that revolved around ethnic and geopolitical positions. Meanwhile, political parties have been efficiently using catch-all and populist methods to attract voters. The death of old political parties and the birth of new ones shortly before elections has become an unwritten tradition, fuelled by individual politicians migrating to new parties along with their alliances.

Within this context, Eurosceptic political parties and individual politicians have emerged as well. Hoping for success similar to that of Eurosceptics in other European Union (EU) countries, individual politicians have put forward the idea of exiting the EU or eurozone. As the election results and polling data demonstrate, and this has been mere

---

K. Bukovskis (✉) • A. Spruds
Latvian Institute of International Affairs, Riga, Latvia
e-mail: karlis.bukovskis@liia.lv; andris.spruds@liia.lv

© The Author(s) 2021
M. Kaeding et al. (eds.), *Euroscepticism and the Future of Europe*,
https://doi.org/10.1007/978-3-030-41272-2_20

wishful thinking. The general sentiment in Latvia is pro-European. Meanwhile, recent years have seen the emergence of EU intergovernmentalist positions in opposition to Latvia's traditional EU-federalist position. One of the central explanations for this is the fact that membership in the EU is a matter of security and geopolitical affiliations for the small Baltic country. Hence, politicians take stances ranging from reason-based federalism or intergovernmentalism to the treason-like *avanteur* of individual Eurosceptic politicians.

There are no Eurosceptic political parties represented in the National Parliament or municipalities. In the May 2019 European Parliament elections, none of the 13 political parties supported leaving the EU. At the same time, several parties expressed dissatisfaction or even anger at the current state of the EU and promised to improve Latvia's socio-economic and political situation in the EU.

Historically, on the 20 September 2003 referendum on Latvia's accession into the European Union, 32.2 percent of voters voted against EU membership. Three political parties were agitators for this, and none of those parties on their own have acquired representation in national or EP elections. The Latvian Socialist Party, however, changed its opinion on the EU and successfully joined an alliance with "Concorde" (Harmony).

Eurosceptic parties are severely marginalized in Latvia. The second agitator is the Eurosceptic Action Party (formerly simply "Eurosceptics") and has also not managed to acquire representation from any municipal, national or EP elections. With only 0.24 percent of the vote in Riga's municipal elections in 2013 and its most visible leader leaving for another political party, the Action Party subsequently "dropped Euroscepticism". This is very similar to the United Social-Democratic Welfare Party, which has been rebranded as the pro-EU "New Harmony" party. Individual politicians have been promoting critical positions on the EU, especially during the most recent bout of Euroscepticism that took place a few years ago, but they have not been successful.

Politicians with an EU intergovernmentalist outlook have become more prominent in the Latvian parliament since the October 2018 national elections. Out of the seven political parties elected, at least three favour slower integration and more national control over the decision-making process. Two of the parties are EU federalists that favour greater powers for the European Commission and European Parliament, and two are somewhat unclear in their positions.

The rising intergovernmentalism trend can be considered as both a belated reaction to the EU membership learning curve, with respect to the rise of critical positions toward the European Commission in Poland and Hungary, as well as an appeal to voters with critical attitudes towards the EU in society. According to the latest Eurobarometer data, approximately 73 percent of Latvia's population views the EU in a positive light, which is a historic high. The rest of the population is less optimistic, however, making them a target for politicians arguing for a reformed, more nation-state-oriented EU, i.e. "a union of nation states".

Eurosceptic parties in Latvia do not affect the government's EU policy as no open Eurosceptics are represented in national institutions. At the same time, parliamentary scrutiny of EU issues, especially by the European Affairs Committee of the Latvian parliament, has become more complex due to the emergence and rising prominence of an "intergovernmentalist wing". The intergovernmentalists acknowledge the political, security and economic impact of Latvia's membership in the EU, but their position towards issues surrounding migration, transatlantic trade and even the future of the EU has been more antagonistic.

Although currently Latvian politicians are not arguing for an exit from the EU or the eurozone, this cannot be excluded, especially considering the increasing living standard, the possible normalization of relations with Russia, the lessening of cohesion funding and the potential rise of charismatic Eurosceptic politicians over the decades to come. As Latvia has seen substantial gains from EU funding and the political and security environment created by EU membership, the overall positive attitude in society towards the EU is understandable and an exit from the EU is seen as treason against national interests.

What Can Be Done? Some Recommendations

First and foremost, the EU and its institutions must be explained in an understandable, appealing and intriguing way. For instance, everyday fun facts about the EU and other Member States published by the European Commission would be helpful. A less diplomatically sanitized and more provocative take on EU practicalities would stir the public's interest. Making the EU entertaining is a must in the modern media environment.

An increasing sense of belongingness and familiarity among Europeans is of the essence. EU wide societal integration and interaction should not be limited to the youth and the Erasmus+ program. EU sport teams consisting of various nationalities would increase a sense of commonness and a sense of pride in the EU and its achievements. Finally, examples of the EU's policy failures should be mentioned to demonstrate how political disagreements do damage to the improvement of living standards.

It can be concluded that Euroscepticism is viewed as treason against Latvia's political, security and economic interests. Meanwhile, a strong EU-federalist approach is also no longer seen as the only option, and pro-federalist politicians are blamed for giving in to the European Commission too much. The recent wave of Euroscepticism in the EU and the emergence of an "intergovernmentalist wing" in Latvia can and must be mitigated. Even reason suggests that the future of the European Union is the future of Europeans.

Liechtenstein: Euroscepticism Yes and No!

Christian Frommelt

There are no Eurosceptic parties in Liechtenstein because all political parties are Eurosceptic. A contradiction? Not really. There are no Eurosceptic parties because Liechtenstein's European policy has hardly been politicised in recent years. All parties support Liechtenstein's membership of the European Economic Area (EEA). This is no surprise if we consider that more than 85 percent of the Liechtenstein citizens have a positive image of the EEA. On the other hand, no party wants to join the European Union (EU) as all of them favour selective integration tailored to Liechtenstein's interests. Consequently, all political parties in Liechtenstein are Eurosceptic.

LIECHTENSTEIN'S ACCESSION TO THE EEA

Liechtenstein voted twice on EEA membership. The first vote took place in December 1992 and the second in April 1995. The second vote was necessary to allow Liechtenstein to join the EEA without jeopardizing the customs union with Switzerland. Both votes were preceded by a fierce debate, although neither party explicitly opposed EEA membership. Instead, opposition to EEA membership came from local industry and

---

C. Frommelt (✉)
Liechtenstein Institut, Bendern, Liechtenstein
e-mail: christian.frommelt@liechtenstein-institut.li

© The Author(s) 2021
M. Kaeding et al. (eds.), *Euroscepticism and the Future of Europe*,
https://doi.org/10.1007/978-3-030-41272-2_21

individual players in the financial centre who organized themselves across party lines. In both votes 56 percent of the people were in favour of EEA membership.

After accession, criticism of the EEA fell silent quickly. One reason for this was certainly the positive effect of EEA membership on the economy. In addition, Liechtenstein was able to continue to control immigration to Liechtenstein through a special solution for the free movement of people. The EU also granted Liechtenstein numerous other opt-outs, which facilitated the administration of EEA membership against the backdrop of the limited resources of Liechtenstein's public administration.

Recent Developments in the Party System

For a long time, Liechtenstein was more or less a two-party system, whereby both the Patriotic Union (VU) and the Progressive Citizens' Party (FBP) positioned themselves in the middle of the political spectrum. It was not until 1993 that a third party, the Free List (FL), and in 2013 a fourth party, the Independents (DU), entered parliament. However, with 16 of the 25 seats available in the Liechtenstein parliament, FBP and VU still have a stable majority.

While the FL can be described as a left-green party, the DU has no clear programme and can therefore hardly be located on a left-right spectrum. In September 2018, three of the five parliamentarians of the DU left their party to create the Democrats for Liechtenstein (DpL). The DpL is the first party in Liechtenstein to position itself clearly to the right of the centre.

The differentiation of the party system is likely to intensify competition in the upcoming elections in 2021. In the struggle for public attention, topics may be politicised that have so far hardly been subject to political debate. This includes European integration, and in one of the first public statements, the DpL had already referred to "foreign determination by Brussels", under which the direct democracy of Liechtenstein "is suffering". The language used by the DpL is very similar to that of the Swiss People's Party (SVP), for which opposition to European integration is crucial.

EEA AS A GAIN OF SOVEREIGNTY?

The Liechtenstein government has always regarded accession to the EEA as a gain in sovereignty. Despite its small size Liechtenstein is equally represented in all EEA EFTA bodies and the EEA provides legal certainty. In addition, EEA membership has enabled Liechtenstein to gain more independence from Switzerland. The narrative of EEA membership as a gain in sovereignty is firmly anchored in the political parties and the public. Recently, however, signs of dissolution became apparent, with Eurosceptics pointing to increasingly dense regulations that are incompatible with the small size of the country, and dwindling flexibility on the part of the EU.

The EEA is therefore no longer immune to criticism in terms of both economic and sovereignty policy. Moreover, if Switzerland and the EU manage to agree on an institutional agreement, some people may see this agreement as an alternative model to EEA membership. It is therefore likely that the EEA and its policies are more often contested in the future.

WHAT CAN BE DONE? SOME RECOMMENDATIONS

Firstly, political parties should not shy away from the debate about the benefits of the EEA for Liechtenstein. The EEA continues to be central to Liechtenstein's businesses and contributes significantly to its reputation as a reliable partner in Europe. It also favours social modernisation in Liechtenstein and improves Liechtenstein's reputation in Europe.

Secondly, political parties should not only focus on the EEA but on European integration in general. Although an EU accession is unlikely in the foreseeable future, the EU's contribution to a politically and economically strong Europe is undoubtable. Therefore, politicians should not play off the EU and EEA against each other by implicitly saying that the EEA is the better model. Those who want to have a well-functioning EEA should also ensure that people have a positive image of the EU.

Thirdly, the manifestos for the next elections should entail topics that have to be addressed at the European level such as climate protection or international trade. In a recent survey conducted in Liechtenstein, security and prosperity were the most frequent associations with Liechtenstein. Due to Liechtenstein's small size these associations are inevitably linked to the success of the EU. However, such topics are often taken for granted and therefore not addressed by political parties.

To conclude, the EEA's achievements are first and foremost EU achievements, in which the EEA/ EFTA States merely participate. As long as the political parties in Liechtenstein are aware of this, it is fair to say that there are no Eurosceptic parties in Liechtenstein, even if no party wants to join the EU.

Lithuania: Euroscepticism—Present on the Margins

Ramūnas Vilpišauskas

In 2019, there were three elections in Lithuania—municipal, presidential and, together with the second round of presidential elections, elections to the European Parliament (EP). The popularly elected president in Lithuania has extensive powers in foreign policy making and executing it, including European policy. Dalia Grybauskaitė who has been in the office for two terms from 2009 to 2019 played a leading role in the country's European affairs. Therefore, the election campaign of 2019 provided a fresh overview of candidates' positions on Lithuania's membership in the European Union (EU).

The main takeaway from the presidential elections was that there was no significant presence of candidates who could be described as Eurosceptic. The one who came closest to such a description was the independent candidate Arvydas Juozaitis who advocated for 'the Europe of nations' and drew media attention by inviting to Vilnius representatives of the Alternative for Germany (AfD) party. However, he came out fifth with

---

R. Vilpišauskas (✉)
Institute of International Relations and Political Science—Vilnius University, Vilnius, Lithuania
e-mail: ramunas.vilpisauskas@tspmi.vu.lt

© The Author(s) 2021
M. Kaeding et al. (eds.), *Euroscepticism and the Future of Europe*,
https://doi.org/10.1007/978-3-030-41272-2_22

only 4.69 per cent of support of participating voters (2.69 per cent of registered voters) and did not make it into the second round of elections. The main candidates, who received the highest support of voters including the winner Gitanas Nausėda, firmly supported Lithuania's membership in the EU by seeing it as beneficial on economics, security and other grounds. The first months of Nausėda's presidency showed a clear tendency for continuity of European policies, previously shown by President Dalia Grybauskaitė and characterised by a focus on security issues, support for Eastern partnership countries' reforms, further integration of infrastructure projects with the rest of the EU and efforts to forge coalitions with neighbouring EU countries.

A similar situation could be observed in the outcomes of the elections in the 2019 European Parliament. It should be noted that the most critical positions of the EU were expressed not only by political parties but by some political movements called public election committees. However, most of the criticism has been vague and stressed constraints imposed by the EU on country's sovereignty without providing more specific details or policy suggestions. The public election committees can participate in the elections in Lithuania alongside the political parties. They have become increasingly popular in the background of a very strong distrust of public opinion in political parties that has been expressed in popular surveys. However, none of them managed to pass the threshold of 5 per cent of votes and were left without any seats in the European Parliament. There was a relatively high voter turnover of 53.48 per cent, most likely due to the second round of presidential elections taking place on the same day. The so-called centrist mainstream parties Homeland Union-Christian Democrats (three seats of the EP) and social-democrats (two seats) came out as the two winners. Behind them were the current ruling party Lithuanian Farmers and Greens Union with two seats. Labour Party, Liberal movement, Alliance of Polish and Russian parties as well as one public elections committee got one seat each. None of them could be described as Eurosceptic.

With the parliamentary elections set for 2020, current opinion polls also show that the public favours mainstream centrist parties which came out as winners in the EP elections. In the current parliament of Lithuania, there are no parties which could be described as Eurosceptic, although some might be cautious with regard to further deepening of the European integration, for example, moving from veto to qualified majority voting in areas of taxation or foreign and security policy. This is a situation that is rather different from other EU member states and calls for possible explanations of the reasons for such a curious absence of politically influential Euroscepticism.

One potential reason has to do with a very high level of popular support for the EU evidenced in opinion surveys such as Eurobarometer. For example, in the 2019 Spring survey the results showed that the trust in the EU in Lithuania was highest of all EU28 member states with 72 per cent of those surveyed in Lithuania indicating their trust in the EU, while the EU average was 44 per cent. In the same survey, 53 per cent of Lithuanians indicated a positive image of the EU, while the EU28 average was 45 per cent. Lithuanians were among the most optimistic of EU28 about the future of the EU with 76 per cent of those surveyed indicating their optimism, while the EU average was 61 per cent. It should be noted that one of the possible explanations for such a positive attitude towards the EU is the possibility to benefit from the free movement of people, including labour since Lithuanians are the most supportive of the free movement of EU citizens of all EU28 member states, 94 per cent indicating their support, while the EU average was 81 per cent. Although emigration to the UK, Ireland, Spain and other EU member states has become a major issue since accession in 2004, freedom of movement is still perceived as a key benefit of EU membership. Besides, visible presence of EU funding for infrastructure and other public investments could also contribute to high popular support of country's EU membership.

Another possible explanation for the high level of popular support for the EU could be linked to the geopolitics, particularly after 2014 when Russia's annexation of Crimea and military conflict with Ukraine received significant media coverage and strengthened concern with the country's security among both political elites and population. Already in mid-1990s when the debate about joining the EU started in Lithuania, security argument for acceding it featured prominently. Although the North Atlantic Treaty Organization (NATO) membership and the presence of the US in Europe are seen as the most important factors for the security of Lithuania, membership in the EU is also seen as enhancing the security of the country.

Therefore, it is probable that political parties and movements which are created for the purpose of participating in the elections follow the public mood and formulate their positions supportive of EU membership. To be sure, current Euroscepticism in most EU member states is rarely linked with advocating withdrawal from the EU. It is rather focused on the reform of the EU to reduce the powers of EU institutions or argues against further deepening of integration. If such a broad definition of Euroscepticism is used, it may be detected in the positions of some political parties such as Order and Justice or Labour Party or segments of the mainstream centrist parties. For example, despite the general consensus that Lithuania had to join all the integration projects such as Schengen and eurozone after acceding to the EU, currently, there is no clearly expressed enthusiasm for further integration in the taxation matters of some other areas where common EU rules might restrict the possibilities for economic catching-up or constrain country's policies such as foreign policy. Interestingly, in the Autumn of 2017 the parliamentary European Affairs Committee initiated a debate on the future of the EU, which was supposed to result in the general position of the parliament. However, after three different position papers were circulated by members of the committee, it proved too difficult to reach a common position because of divergent views towards the further deepening of integration.

What Can Be Done? Some Recommendations

To conclude, although the support among political parties in Lithuania for further deepening of integration is not as strong as it was for joining the EU (in May 2003, out of 63.4 per cent of voters who came to vote, 91.1 per cent supported EU membership), the parties and political movements which could be described as Eurosceptic remain marginal in terms of popular support and their input into the political debates on the future of the EU. Their presence has become more visible, and they are more vocal in expressing their views, particularly in the debates on politics of memory and symbols of national identity. However, they have not made any significant impact on the Lithuanian official position regarding the EU or public trust in the EU. However, current relatively high support for the EU membership seems somewhat at odds with the tendency of a significant share of voters to regularly shift towards supporting newly created political movements, which could be characterised as populist, during each parliamentary election. This seems to point towards negative motivation of trusting the EU which could be linked to very low trust in national political institutions (and a very low interpersonal trust). Strong support for the EU might change if, for example, security concerns in the region become less important or financial EU support decreases significantly. Therefore, there is a need for a genuine public debate on the pros and cons of further integration which has been less pronounced in the last decade.

Luxembourg: Make Europe Work Better in the Greater Regions

Guido Lessing

In the last general election, held in October 2018, the Luxembourgish electorate confirmed the incumbent coalition government of the liberal Democratic Party (DP), the Greens (Déi Gréng) and the Luxembourg Socialist Workers' Party (LSAP). The government majority, composed entirely of pro-European parties, lost just one seat. The most Eurosceptic party represented in the national parliament, the Alternative Democratic Reform Party (ADR), obtained 8.28 percent of the votes cast (compared with 6.64 percent in 2013) and gained one more seat in the Chamber of Deputies. In the current legislature, it holds 4 out of 60 seats. Although the ADR received more votes than in the previous elections, from the party's perspective the result was somewhat disappointing. In Luxembourg, unlike in its neighbouring countries, the European migrant crisis of 2015 has not led to a significant surge of right-wing, anti-European forces.

Another factor also turned out to be less favourable for the ADR than expected. In June 2015, Luxembourg held a constitutional referendum,

---

G. Lessing (✉)
Luxembourg Centre for Contemporary and Digital History,
Esch-sur-Alzette, Luxembourg
e-mail: guido.lessing@ext.uni.lu

with one of the questions being the issue of the right of foreigners to vote. The proponents hoped that this would enable Luxembourg's democracy to adapt to the reality of a society composed of almost 50 percent of foreign nationals, predominantly EU migrants. Much to the surprise of the governing parties, which campaigned for foreigners' right to vote, the result was devastating. Almost 80 percent of Luxembourgish voters rejected the idea. In the aftermath of the referendum, the ADR successfully courted the initiators of an original non-partisan social media campaign that had been launched in opposition to the extension of voting rights. It hoped to benefit from the popularity of these social media campaigners by adding them as candidates on the party's electoral list, but the election results revealed that this strategy was not a great success for the ADR. The referendum really proved to have been a single-issue vote and not a plebiscite against the incumbent (pro-European) government.

Just seven months after the general election, voters were again called upon to cast their votes in May 2019, this time to elect Luxembourg's six MEPs in the 751-strong European Parliament. None of the ADR candidates was elected, nor those of any other Eurosceptic party running for the European elections in Luxembourg. However, the tides of Euroscepticism are difficult to assess solely on the grounds of the two most recent election results. First, in a country of slightly more than 600,000 inhabitants, where voters often know candidates personally, ideological differences tend to play a lesser role in voting behaviour than they do in larger countries. Moreover, in Luxembourg, voters can allocate their votes either to single candidates or to party lists. This led to a de facto threshold of more than 12 percent for parties to send their candidates to the European Parliament. Second, although only Luxembourgish nationals enjoy the right to vote in general elections, European elections are open to all EU nationals. In this context, it important to recall that non-Luxembourgers represent almost half of the resident population. Third, voting is mandatory for Luxembourgish citizens. Consequently, voter turnout is generally around 90 percent of registered voters, but in 2019 only 12 percent of non-Luxembourgish EU citizens registered to vote in the elections for the EP.

As the results of the 2019 EP elections in Luxembourg suggest, more than 10 percent of the electorate are Eurosceptic. Fundamental criticism comes from both edges of the political spectrum. The Communist Party (2019: 1.14 percent) and the Left (Déi Lénk, 2019: 4.84 percent) criticize the neo-liberal orientation of EU policy. The ADR takes a sovereigntist stance and defends by its own accounts the idea of a "Europe of Nations". Since 2010, the party has been a member of the Eurosceptic Alliance of Conservatives and Reformists in Europe (ACRE), without ever having gained a seat in the European Parliament. 10.04 percent of votes cast for the ADR in 2019 were not sufficient to send a candidate to Strasbourg.

The evolution of ADR from a single-issue party to a Eurosceptic, sovereigntist party is closely linked to the at least partially shared feeling of alienation in a multilingual and multicultural society. In this context, the Luxembourgish language as a vector of national identity has significantly gained in importance. In 2018, the government therefore launched an action plan to promote Luxembourgish as a vehicle of communication (besides the country's two other official languages, French and German) and to make Luxembourgish one of the official languages of the European Union. This is partly a reaction to the ADR's vocal claim that the Luxembourgish language should be reassessed at European level, especially in light of the recognition of other small European languages such as Irish and Maltese as official EU languages.

Traditionally, the Luxembourgish government has taken a pro-European stance combined with a determination to defend its vital economic interests. As Luxembourg is a highly integrated economy, dependent on the single market, any solitary political impulses would be highly damaging. The leaders of the ADR are well aware of this fact, and yet the party has repeatedly referred to its ideological and political proximity to the UK Conservative Party. At a parliamentary hearing in November 2018, the most well-known ADR politician on European affairs, Fernand Kartheiser, congratulated the British people on Brexit, whereas all the other political parties expressed deep regret at the United Kingdom's decision to leave the European Union. So far, Eurosceptic positions have not gained any significance in Luxembourg's EU policy. On the contrary, the furious reaction of the long-standing Luxembourg Minister of Foreign Affairs, Jean Asselborn, to the disparaging remarks of the then Italian Minister of the Interior, Matteo Salvini, on African migrants at an informal meeting in September 2018 stirred much sympathy for the Luxembourg minister among the wider public. Shortly after this, a quote from his vocal outburst ("Merde alors") was printed on T-shirts and marketed with some success. However, as an advocate of a common European redistribution mechanism for migrants, Asselborn has become a major target of mockery and scorn from the Eurosceptic ADR.

What Can Be Done? Some Recommendations

In recent years, public discourse on the EU has been increasingly dominated by its real or supposed failures. Developing another discourse which points to the achievements of the European integration project is a major challenge. From the Luxembourgish point of view, this means fostering awareness of the degree of integration already reached, especially with regard to the Greater Region (composed of the Grand Duchy of Luxembourg, Wallonia, Saarland, Lorraine, Rhineland-Palatinate and the German-speaking community of Belgium), where European integration is lived out on a daily basis. Since the single market and its open borders are also associated with uncontrolled growth and widespread housing and infrastructure problems, the government should respond actively to these challenges and find solutions across national borders. Their approach should include all aspects of work, education, health and recreation. At the same time, future EU enlargement plans should be considered with caution. From a Luxembourgish perspective, priority should be given to a period of consolidation in a Union exposed to strong centrifugal forces.

Malta: Bucking the Trend—How Malta Turned its Back on Euroscepticism

Mark Harwood

Malta has followed a unique trajectory in terms of Euroscepticism, being the only country of the 2004 accession states where a major party and nearly 50 percent of voters were opposed to EU (European Union) membership pre-2004. Fifteen years later the country's party system is now overwhelmingly Euro-enthusiastic. The Maltese show some of the highest approval ratings for the EU and Malta's place in the Union. As in all European Parliament (EP) elections held since 2004, in 2019 Malta again registered the highest turnout for a country where voting is not obligatory and distributed its 6 seats amongst the S&D (Progressive Alliance of Socialists and Democrats) (4 seats) and the EPP (European People's Party) (2 seats). Malta is now one of the few EU countries with no Eurosceptic parties in Parliament.

Several factors can be brought forward to explain this situation. Malta's hard Euroscepticism manifested pre-accession was a reflection of its polarised party system. Since 1966 only 2 parties have sat in parliament and the duopoly of power enjoyed by the Social Democrats (on the left) and

M. Harwood (✉)
Institute for European Studies, University of Malta, Msida, Malta
e-mail: mark.harwood@um.edu.mt

Christian Democrats (on the right) means that almost all major issues become politicised and polarised (a third party entered parliament in 2017, but as part of an electoral coalition with the Christian Democrats and can be considered an extension of the two-party system). From 1990 onwards this included the question of EU membership, which the Social Democrats opposed due to fears that membership would compromise the country's neutrality and undermine its economy in the face of market liberalisation. However, this form of hard Euroscepticism was not critical of the EU but of Malta's place in the Union. With no principled opposition to European integration, Eurobarometer surveys have always shown the Maltese expressing above-average support for the Union as an institution, if not Malta's place in it.

Once the Maltese voted in favour of joining in the 2003 referendum (53 percent voted in favour, 47 percent opposed) and then re-affirmed this decision in the ensuing general election of 2003 (with the Christian Democrats winning), the Social Democrats took a formal decision to reverse their opposition to EU membership and from this point on, Malta turned its back on party-based Euroscepticism. The Christian Democrats (in power until 2013) have seen EU membership as one of their greatest achievements while the Social Democrats have no wish to politicise membership; the party's old guard still has lingering, Eurosceptic feelings and the 2008 and 2013 party manifestos included commitments to reverse some EU policies (Dublin II) but the party has increasingly framed much of its progressive social agenda as the attainment of 'European rights'.

On the periphery of the party system, minor parties have emerged, but they do not challenge the two-party system, never having managed to secure a seat in national or EP elections. Malta's Single Transferable Voting system (STV) imposes a 15 percent threshold on candidates which makes it almost impossible to break the duopoly. Of the smaller parties, the Greens have been the most consistently pro-EU (contesting elections since the 1990s) while far-right parties soon emerged after EU membership, as irregular migration from North Africa also started. Of these, three are of note. The Alliance for Change (Alleanza Bidla) is socially conservative and the most pointedly anti-EU. The Maltese Patriots are primarily anti-migrant but also opposed to fundamentals of EU integration such as free movement while the Imperium Europa is the most blatantly fascist of the fringe parties being deeply racist and committed to 'An Imperium for Europids (where) the travesty of democracy will have no place'. None of these far-right parties have gained more than 1 percent in national elections though the Imperium Europa has performed well in EP elections, securing 3 percent of the vote in the 2019 election. This is insignificant when compared to the 15 percent needed in EP elections (14 percent to 16 percent in national elections, depending on the district) to secure a seat but is enough for it to claim it is the third biggest party in Malta.

While Euroscepticism has been side-lined, nationalistic themes have been gaining ground. The 2019 European elections saw one of the most negative campaigns in Europe and focused squarely on the issue of patriotism and allegations of corruption within the machinery of government. Beyond this narrow focus, elements within the Christian Democrats have been flirting with xenophobia. Some argue that it is a lazy attempt to grab the far-right vote; with a booming economy and the largest population growth in Europe in recent years, more and more pressure is mounting on the island with spiralling house prices, mounting pressure on the country's free education and health system and an explosion in construction. It has become easy to pander to an increasingly xenophobic subgroup though, as one minister said, it is difficult to politicise success and with the country's economic growth remaining strong, this subgroup is likely to remain on the fringe and with this in mind, it is not surprising to note that there has been little impact of Eurosceptic rhetoric on government EU policy. While the country has consistently called for burden sharing in migration, its priority remains a commitment to oppose EU tax harmonisation and, to a lesser degree, minimise the likelihood of the country becoming a net-contributor to the EU budget in the near future, but this is more about maintaining the status quo. Should the Government decide to tackle right-wing, xenophobic Euroscepticism from emerging, they would do well to provide clearer media campaigns explaining the importance of incoming migration, prioritise teaching about the EU in schools (to counter misinformation) and prioritise inclusion programmes, for the Maltese as well as foreign residents. In the long term, Malta should continue to oppose efforts to create a federal Europe, something which the Maltese, in general, oppose.

What Can Be Done? Some Recommendations

Malta's experience of Euroscepticism gives limited potential for making recommendations for other countries; its highly polarised, two-party system was a primary factor in the emergence of Euroscepticism pre-accession but once party-based opposition was abandoned and with continuing economic success, there is limited potential for Europe to become a divisive issue in domestic politics. That said, with the European Union losing a key ally (the UK), the country will soon become a net contributor and with the European Union entering areas of further cooperation with the potential to harm Malta's interests (in particular with tax harmonisation), there is nothing to say that it cannot re-emerge as an issue in the future.

Montenegro: A Great Bargain Between the European Union Optimism and Real Euroscepticism

Danijela Jaćimović and Sunčica Rogic

The European integration process has been the most powerful engine for overall change in Montenegro over the last two decades. The integration process has become a key motivating factor behind the country's economic and political reforms.

European Union (EU) membership is the most important foreign policy priority for Montenegro, and one which all parliamentary parties agree on. This makes Montenegro one of the rare countries in Europe, where no political party is explicitly against European integration and there is a strong consensus between the political parties about the strategic importance of this process. The makeup of the Montenegrin parliament, based on the most recent parliamentary elections that were held in 2016, are as follows: the Democratic Party of Socialists (DPS which have 36 seats, Democratic Front (DF) that holds 18 seats, the Grand Coalition KEY with 9 seats (this coalition is composed of the following political parties: DEMOS, the Socialist People's Party SPP and United Reform Action

---

D. Jaćimović (✉) • S. Rogic
Faculty of Economics, University of Montenegro, Podgorica, Montenegro
e-mail: danijelaj@ucg.ac.me; suncica@ucg.ac.me

© The Author(s) 2021
M. Kaeding et al. (eds.), *Euroscepticism and the Future of Europe*,
https://doi.org/10.1007/978-3-030-41272-2_25

URA), the Democrats of Montenegro (DCG) have 8 seats, the Social Democrats (SD) hold 2 seats, and the Social Democratic Party of Montenegro (SDP) have 4 seats. Furthermore, minority parties representing some of the main minority ethnic groups in Montenegro are also represented in parliament. Thus, the Bosniak Party (BS) has 2 seats, while the Albanian Party and the Croatian Civic Initiative both have 1 seat each. The current ruling coalition consists of three parties: The Democratic Party of Socialists (lead by Milo Đukanovic), the Social Democrats (whose leader is Ivan Brajovic) and the Bosniak party (whose leader is Rafet Husovic).

This political agreement represents an accomplishment, considering that most of the current political parties were outspoken in their anti-Western orientation during the 1990s. The key driver behind Montenegro's foreign policy shift towards the EU has been the position of the Democratic Party of Socialist (DPS), which has dominated politics in Montenegro over the last thirty years. Moreover, the process has been driven in particular by Đukanović's own personal decisions.

Behind this political consensus there is also a strong EU orientation of the Montenegrin citizens, who consider themselves Europeans and believe that the EU (and the West) is the natural place where they should live and work. Moreover, there is a strong belief that future EU membership will increase standards in all areas, and lead Montenegrin society towards prosperity. Despite the many changes that the EU has experienced over the last decade, the basic attractiveness of this process for Montenegrin citizens has not been altered. According to the latest Eurobarometer report, 63 percent of Montenegrin citizens strongly support the EU integration. At the same time, all the political parties have essentially left-wing roots, and these are some of the most powerful reasons why there is not much evident right wing/ Eurosceptic rhetoric in Montenegro. Thus, we can conclude that there is little clear and open Euroscepticism on the Montenegrin political scene.

The most recent EU parliamentary elections in 2019 had only a limited impact on domestic politics in Montenegro. The domestic political parties have only limited communication with their European political party peers, notably through the Parliamentary Committee for Stabilization and Association established in 2010. Meanwhile, only two parties are member of European party groupings: the DPS and the SDP, who are also members of the Socialist International, while most of the opposition parties are not yet members of any European or internationally recognized political party association.

Given that Montenegro is a small country, it has a political system that is often affected by certain very important external or foreign forces. This is more than evident in the way that the political parties address North Atlantic Treaty Organization (NATO) membership, which was achieved by Montenegro in 2017. Most opposition parties are against NATO membership, and, in many cases, these are the same parties that were strongly against independence in 2006. In their rhetoric we can find certain elements of Eurosceptic or anti-Western argument. During the parliamentary elections in 2016, Democratic Front pronounced clear forms of Eurosceptic rhetoric as regards to Montenegro's potential membership and especially the future of the EU more generally. This represented a novelty on the domestic political scene, but it has not had a particularly strong impact on voters, and there is no growing trend of public support for this anti-Western and anti-EU orientation.

When we talk about critical issues or policy areas such as corruption, reform fatigue, enlargement fatigue, (e)migration and expectation management regarding the EU accession process. The key role is taken by the government and its dialogue with the EU Delegation and EU Member Countries. The impact of the opposition political parties has been very limited, even for those that use Eurosceptic arguments, and any effect has been more about addressing domestic voters and their political priorities and less interested in shaping particular public policies. It is interesting that the media and some NGO organizations have filled this gap, and sometimes act much more effectively than opposition political parties in (re)shaping public policies.

What Can Be Done? Some Recommendations

The extent of the challenges in negotiating EU accession has caused a very slow process in practical terms for Montenegro (which has one of the longest negotiations in European history, having started in 2012). This means there is no clear view of the end of the process. This in itself would suggest that changes are very needed. Countries in the Western Balkans are faced by a significant number of different internal and external issues and require different approaches, instruments and time. These factors influence the integration processes of each country, which in general terms should perhaps be more political and less technical. Rethinking instruments to move away from a "one size fits all" would be a good start and might prove vital in keeping reform alive. It is evident that mentality also plays an important role in terms of reform implementation, while some reforms simply need more time and more gradualism, which suggests that "fast track" reforms are not performing well and may in fact be counterproductive.

North Macedonia: The Name in Exchange for European Union Membership?

Irena Rajchinovska Pandeva

North Macedonia is, in all probability, the poster country for the reluctant enlargement policy by the European Union (EU) towards the Western Balkans (WB). Due to a concoction of internal and external issues, over the past years the country was left standing still at the intersection of an alignment with the West or seclusion to the regional conundrum. North Macedonia became a candidate country for EU accession in 2005 as a frontrunner in the WB and pledged to follow the accession agenda, so the EU became highly involved into its daily politics equally by the process of integration and the membership conditionality. The first recommendation for the start of accession negotiations was announced in 2009, and even though it was followed by subsequent recommendations by the European Commission, the Council's conclusion in October 2019 was a negative one. The decision not to open negotiations due to the objection of a few member states, most predominantly France, provoked a serious anti-EU sentiment in North Macedonia, and, beyond everything, a resentment since it was openly associated with the notion that the name was sacrificed

---

I. Rajchinovska Pandeva (✉)
Faculty of Law Iustinianus Primus, Ss. Cyril and Methodus University, Skopje, North Macedonia

in exchange for the EU accession. The reaction was widespread and intense and even led to the decision to have early parliamentary elections. In addition to the impact on national affairs, this outcome has disregarded the promise of EU enlargement policy in the WB, and North Macedonia in particular, and may challenge its stability and security, to such an extent that the impending North Atlantic Treaty Organization (NATO) membership, assurances of economic support and cooperation and EU regional and national presence cannot balance them out.

This sensitivity originates from the resilient and deep-rooted tenacity of Macedonia's EU agenda since the country gained independence in 1991. Up to now, its public opinion has demonstrated an unbalanced approach towards the advantages and pitfalls of EU accession, by putting the weight only on the gains related mostly to economic progress and welfare. This viewpoint has been pushed forward by the key political parties in North Macedonia from the onset. The general apprehension of EU accession barely takes into account the complexity of the EU and the main issues that give rise to Euroscepticism, populism, nationalism and distrust among EU citizens. The Macedonian distinct path towards the EU and NATO is paved by 27 years of protracted negotiations over the name issue, regional unresolved disputes, political instability and ambiguous security. Therefore, successive political elites have bestowed EU and NATO integration as the bright light at the end of the tunnel, which by the end of 2019 encompassed a change of the official name of the Republic, resolving all open disputes with its immediate neighbourhood, alteration of the national identity narrative and closure of the inter-ethnic issues. As follows, the closure of the name issue was asserted as the final obstacle on EU integration (both by internal and external actors), so the consent for the erga-omnes use of the new name was in a way a vote for European North Macedonia.

The Prespa Agreement and the 2018 referendum stirred up the political arena, so a number of existing and newly flourished political parties and groups gave rise to the opposition on the brokered deal. A markedly hostile reception was met by VMRO DPMNE as a main opposition party, the President of the Republic, a significant part of the ethnic Macedonians and the intellectual elite. In view of that, it came as no surprise that the political landscape was enriched by the spur of right and far right groups such as Tvrdokorni, Edinstvena Makedonija and so on. These groups, marginal as they may be, put forward the idea that EU and NATO integration has an alternative and Macedonia has even greater allies, such as Russia. The ambivalent attitude towards the Russian influence is most likely a result of the protracted EU integration of the country which is why the polls over the past years show a rise and fall interplay between the EU and Russia as the greatest allies of North Macedonia.

The SDSM party rhetorically and policy wise, since it holds the Government seat, supports the EU (and the USA) as the country's most significant allies. The main opposition party, VMRO-DPMNE, in terms of rhetoric, endorses the advance towards EU and NATO, while in terms of political activity it utilizes a fluctuating stand often sending out a mixed political message. At the peak of Gruevski's reign, the VMRO-DPMNE-led government managed to create a very strong anti-EU sentiment when needed and used the country's failure to align with the EU and NATO as an argument to justify active policies or pass on responsibility for failed ones. Conversely, the SDSM-led government spent almost three years focusing mostly on external affairs and neglecting the extant problems of the country and accumulating even more. Despite the proclaimed determination to push forward reform processes by a series of action plans, the high-level corruption scandals, including the "Racket" extortion scandal—involving the Special Public Prosecutor's office itself—in addition to many more, proved that the rule of law, reforming the judiciary and separation of powers are a prerequisite for development and can be exploited for denial of EU accession. The ethnic Albanian political parties—DUI, BESA, DPA and Alliance for Albanians—still show a high and steady support for the EU and NATO integration, but the abuse of EU agenda by them is also very present and has been employed by all of them and DUI especially.

During the past decade, the heavy involvement by the international community and above all by the EU, in North Macedonia, has created a unique setting for parallel development of regression from within and interference from the outside. Remarkably, the EU involvement has been largely disapproved by both sides of the political spectrum: SDSM has criticized the EU for late acknowledgement of the state capture only in 2016, while VMRO-DPMNE has criticized the EU for its role in brokering the erga-omnes name resolution. So, if we were to locate indications of Euroscepticism in North Macedonia within the mainstream political arena prior to October 2019, these are the realms we should be looking at.

What Can Be Done? Some Recommendations

Taming the most expected Euroscepticism in North Macedonia after the 2019 Brussels' fiasco will require genuine attestation on its EU prospect which can only materialize by opening the negotiation talks promptly and with no further delays. The international community must recognize that no other option can replace its EU prospects, not at least the compromise of privileged partnership as a substitute for full membership or economic integration instead of political according to the latest backup option. The closed EU door will reinforce its immigration flow, mainly towards EU states, and will endanger the implementation of bilateral agreements linked to its EU accession (foremost the Prespa Agreement). Additionally, it will neutralize pro-European agents and give leverage to the anti-European populists across the political spectrum and Euroscepticism will be higher than its 2008 level, after the NATO Bucharest Summit. The disappointment will most likely diminish the credibility of the EU as a project, make the integration process and policy less plausible and forfeit the influence of the EU as a key external mediator since this time around scepticism and the revival of the myth of victimization will be higher, and this is by far one of the most dangerous scenarios for the Balkans.

Norway: Outside, But …

John Erik Fossum

Norway applied for membership in the European Union (EU) four times, in the 1960s, 1970s and 1990s. The first two instances, in 1962 and 1967, were aborted due to de Gaulle's veto against the UK's application. In connection with the two next applications, in 1972 and 1994, the EU membership question was voted over in popular referendums that were arranged after the negotiations had been completed. In both instances, a small majority of the population turned down EU membership (in 1972, 53.5 per cent voted against membership and 46.5 per cent voted for, and in 1994, 52.2 per cent voted against, whereas 47.8 per cent voted in favour).

The question of Norwegian EU membership has figured as one of, if not, the most politically divisive issues in Norway, at least since the Second World War. The question of EU membership has reawakened and given added impetus to old and entrenched cleavages—the urban-rural and centre-periphery cleavages that go back centuries. When the EU membership issue came on the agenda, the EU-friendly political centre in Oslo was pitted against Eurosceptic peripheries in the West and the North; and Eurosceptic rural areas were pitted against less Eurosceptic urban areas. The EU membership question divided the political scene in yes and no parties. The most EU-friendly party was the Conservative Party (Høyre,

---

J. E. Fossum (✉)
ARENA—Centre for European Studies, Oslo, Norway
e-mail: j.e.fossum@arena.uio.no

© The Author(s) 2021
M. Kaeding et al. (eds.), *Euroscepticism and the Future of Europe*,
https://doi.org/10.1007/978-3-030-41272-2_27

which got 25 per cent of the vote in the 2017 national election) with a strong urban base, whereas the most Eurosceptic party was the Centre Party (which got 10.3 per cent of the vote in the 2017 election), with a strong rural and agricultural base. The largest party, the Social Democrats (AP, which got 27.4 per cent in the 2017 election), has for most of the time been split with a rough 60/40 divide in favour of EU membership, whereas the Left Socialist Party (what is now Sosialistisk Venstreparti, got 6 per cent of the votes in the 2017 election) has always been against EU membership. It is interesting to note that the populist right-wing party, the Progress Party (Fremskrittspartiet, which got 15.2 per cent of the votes in the 2017 election), has historically speaking been nowhere near as Eurosceptic as has generally been the case with the right-wing populist party family it belongs to (Euroscepticism is a hallmark of such comparable parties as the Danish People's Party or the French National Rally). For a long time, the party (knowing it was internally divided) sought to keep the EU issue off the agenda. In the last few years, though, the party has become more explicitly Eurosceptic, in connection with its anti-immigration ethnic nationalism, which places an onus on confining welfare benefits to Norwegian nationals. Even if it has stated a commitment to renegotiate Schengen and (was during the period October 16, 2013 until January 24, 2020 one of the governing parties, it is not likely to initiate such a process (it is currently polling at 10.3 per cent).

What is important to underline is that although the people rejected Norwegian EU membership in two referenda, Norway is today heavily Europeanized. Norway is associated with the EU through more than 130 agreements, ranging from the internal market, the Schengen association agreement, agreements on asylum and police cooperation (Dublin I, II and III), agreements on foreign and security policy (Norway participates in the EU's battle groups) and agreements on internal security and justice. Through these agreements, Norway has incorporated roughly three-quarters of EU legislation compared to those EU member states that have incorporated everything. In effect, Norway's approach has been to seek as close an EU association as is possible for a non-member. Norway's EU contribution (including EFTA 50 million Euros for Norway's EFTA membership) is 890 million Euros per year. Assessed in terms of per capita, Norway's contribution is less than two-thirds of the UK's (£ 140 per person in Norway and £ 220 per person in the UK).

This emphasis on as close as possible an EU association as is basically possible for a non-member is very interesting given that the main argument of the no side was that EU membership would undermine Norwegian sovereignty and democracy. It is clear that Norway's current close EU affiliation has profound implications for Norwegian constitutional democracy. Some would even say that those that voted no won at the day of the referendum (28 November 1994) but have lost every day since.

In these circumstances, what is particularly puzzling is that the present situation has evoked so little political conflict and controversy. Norway, despite being deeply divided over the question of EU membership, has faithfully adopted and incorporated EU laws and regulations throughout the EEA Agreement's life. Parties in government, whether they are in favour or against EU membership, have all the same incorporated a vast body of EU laws and regulations without any real ability to effect these.

Some have argued that Norway's no to EU membership was due to distinct cultural factors that set it apart from those states that embraced EU membership. Such a claim is difficult to square with the fact that Norway is very similar to its Nordic EU member neighbours, is so closely affiliated with the EU and, no less importantly, that this democratically problematic form of affiliation has provoked so little political controversy. Had Norway been so culturally distinct as some of the most vocal Eurosceptics claimed, we would have seen strong and explicit instances of political mobilization bent on cultural preservation. Instead, what we find is an ongoing, dynamic and very comprehensive process of EU adaptation that has run for well over 25 years (since the EEA Agreement came into effect in 1994), without any ruptures and where the reservation right built into the EEA Agreement has never been triggered.

We cannot really understand this situation without focusing on how the Norwegian political system and especially the political parties have behaved. What is important to note is that the political parties have instituted informal rules and arrangements to keep the EU membership issue off the political agenda. All governments are (some version of) coalition governments, because the proportional electoral system favours middle-sized parties and makes it difficult for any one party to gain a majority of seats. Since there are EU-supporting (notably the Conservative Party and Labour) and EU-opposing parties (notably the Centre Party, the Left Socialist Party, Red (Rødt, with 2.4 per cent of the vote in the 2017 election), the Liberal Party (Venstre, with 4.4 per cent of the vote in the 2017 election) and the Christian People's Party (KrF, with 4.2 per cent of the vote in the 2017 election)) on both sides of the left to right scale, it means effectively that all coalitions have to consist of parties favouring Norwegian

EU membership (even if internally divided) as well as parties opposing EU membership. Most of the parties, with the exception of the Centre Party and Red, are basically in support of the EEA Agreement. As part of the coalition agreement—whether explicitly stated or tacitly agreed—the parties commit themselves to retain the present EU affiliation. Efforts to change the status quo effectively mean that the coalition unravels; hence, a party has to weigh the merits of remaining in government against the merits of altering Norway's status in relation to the EU. When the EU membership issue is off the agenda, it is much easier for parties to live with an ongoing process of adopting EU norms and rules. The cumulative effects of EU adaptation become less visible because EU adaptation is effectively disaggregated into a stream of individual measures. This situation makes it easier to maintain the perception of national independence even if the reality is ongoing incorporation—self-chosen submission—under EU rules and norms.

The formal status as a non-member coupled with the credo of as close an affiliation as possible is presented as a national compromise. It is understood as the price that EU supporters must pay for retaining EU access and the price that EU opponents must pay for retaining formal sovereignty. This bundle of informal political agreements has made it possible for coalitions that are deeply divided on EU membership to stay together and operate a society that is becoming increasingly Europeanized. It is unlikely that this arrangement would have been sustainable had it not been for a range of other factors such as a consensus-oriented and consultative political system and a well-functioning public sector, which enjoys high levels of public trust, bolstered by a comprehensive welfare-state that buffers people from the predicaments of a rapidly changing world. These factors are closely linked to a progressive public program of gender equality. The political compromise is thus sustained by important socio-economic factors.

What Can Be Done? Some Recommendations

The question that Brexit brings up is how resilient Norway's EU arrangement is when there are other affiliation models in play. Norway's current EU affiliation has considerable popular support, as is shown in a string of opinion polls. At the same time, there are critical voices across the political spectrum, and there may be a greater willingness to consider alternatives. Thus far, we see that EEA opponents are struggling to come up with clear alternatives. Well before the Brexit referendum, there was talk about the Swiss model, but the EU is unlikely to accept that. In any case, the Swiss model leaves Switzerland with less actual leverage than what appears from the formal arrangement. EU membership is an obvious alternative but there is very little support for that. This suggests that Brexit would be the place to look for alternatives and thus far Brexit's unfolding has served mainly to deter people from opting for a looser EU affiliation.

In Norway, the core of Euroscepticism has historically been rural-agrarian hostility to urban-industrial/post-industrial development. There was nevertheless an important change between 1972 and 1994 when Euroscepticism became more focused on protecting the public sector and the welfare state both of which were seen as guarantors of gender equality. In other words, Norwegian Euroscepticism took on a hostility to neo-liberalism. The lesson from Norway is that if the EU continues along the neo-liberal track, it will breed Euroscepticism because this sentiment cuts across the entire political spectre.

Poland: Economic Enthusiasts, Value Adversaries

Zdzisław Mach and Natasza Styczyńska

Having a right-wing Eurosceptic coalition in power led by Law and Justice party (PiS) might come as a surprise because Poles are one of the most pro-European societies in the European Union (EU). According to recent opinion polls (COBOS 2019), 91 per cent of Polish society declare to be positive about EU membership, and only 5 per cent think Poland shouldn't be part of the EU.

The Polish political arena has shifted to the right and during the last term of the parliament (2015–2019), there was not a single left-wing party represented in the Sejm. The right-wing—as elsewhere in Europe— opposes deeper European integration, and some parties like the radical National Movement are openly anti-EU. Ethnic nationalism plays an important role in shaping the political agenda of these parties and right-wing organisations. According to this stance, the nation is understood as an ethnic concept and a community of people who think alike. This brings the notion of a closed homogenous society which finds it difficult to accept any kind of otherness and is unwilling to welcome newcomers, especially if they are of a different religion or race.

Z. Mach • N. Styczyńska (✉)
Institute of European Studies, Jagiellonian University, Krakow, Poland
e-mail: zdzislaw.mach@uj.edu.pl; natasza.styczynska@uj.edu.pl

In the Polish version, ethnic nationalism is strongly supported by the Catholic Church, which is seen as the guardian of Polish identity which combines ethnic heritage with Catholicism. However, the Church has never spoken univocally on the subject of European integration. There are many factions, from those strongly critical of Western Europe to others which are socially liberal and dialogue-oriented. The official position of the Church regarding Poland's integration to the EU was positive, but nowadays the voice of the Church is dominated by those who hold Europe accountable for the spreading of decadence and the "civilisation of death", as well as the so-called "LGBT ideology". This tendency is increasing, with a strong cooperation between the conservative clergy, bishops and the ruling Law and Justice party.

In Poland a historically developed self-perception of the nation is noticed by being continuously under threat and oppressed by other nations and always suffering but morally victorious. Consequently, the relations with other nations are primarily seen from the perspective of potential danger for national identity and sovereignty. This logic is also applied to relations with the EU that is perceived as an external body which may be useful but to which the Poles do not see themselves as belonging. Many Poles believe that the help from the EU is deserved because of their past suffering and heroism and as compensation for communist oppression, rather than perceiving it as an investment in the common future. Hence the overwhelming support for membership may be interpreted as a desire to continue benefiting from being in the EU but does not reflect any sense of belonging to the European community of values or the presence of a common European identity. Now, 15 years after the enlargement, mainstream Polish Euroscepticism in its essence is a reduction of the EU strictly into economic cooperation, which would still allow for the redistribution of funds for the benefit of poorer nations but would not extend to the European public sphere, civil society and common European identity. The ruling coalition avoids discussing Europe in detail, limiting themselves to the use of the slogan "Poland, the heart of Europe". In their discourse, the EU is portrayed as a source of economic profit, while the identity or value dimension is lacking.

In 2015, PiS used the fear of the others (asylum seekers) in their parliamentary campaign in order to garner support. Also, the ongoing dispute with the European Commission over the rule of law serves as an example of what kind of EU the ruling party wants. The EU has no right to intervene in the domestic affairs of its members—big member states such as Germany are accused of having too much control. The follow-up argument points out the current condition of the EU, which is in crisis and should not teach its member states before solving its own issues. According to Eurosceptic nationalists, Europe has gone mad and is showing suicidal tendencies by accepting the "others" whose only aim is to destroy Europe. This dangerous and self-destructive inclination is due to the dominant left-wing liberalism. Saving "real Europe" that is based on Christian values could be the task for countries such as Poland or other Eastern European member states. This type of narrative was also visible during the 2019 European Parliamentary (EP) elections that were won by PiS, as part of the European Conservatives and Reformists group in the EP. 4.5 percent of the votes went to the xenophobic and anti-European right-wing Konfederacja, which didn't make it to the EP because of the 5 per cent threshold.

This type of rhetoric seems to appeal to young Polish citizens as it easily explains their frustrations. This is especially true of those members of the society, not only the youth but of those who think of themselves as victims of the post-communist transformation. Those suffering from a loss of ontological security, who do not understand and are not able to cope with the various challenges, and those who search for a kind of simple explanation of the open, changing world which they fear. Tradition and strong national leadership may seem to be a good solution, by providing them simple answers to difficult questions and easy distinctions between good and evil, naming enemies responsible for their misfortunes and bringing hope for a better future.

WHAT CAN BE DONE? SOME RECOMMENDATIONS

From the point of view of the integration of Poland into the EU, the main mistake was already made during the first years after the enlargement. This mistake was the belief that if institutional mechanisms of democracy and the free market are implemented, the Europeanisation of all the other spheres of society would follow automatically. This, as we see now, did not happen. More investment in education and culture is needed as well as more emphasis on shaping and creating the feeling of belonging to the European community of values. If the EU wants to change the situation for member states which have turned onto the illiberal path, it should insist on keeping European values and not consider any compromises over them with the Eurosceptic governments. A very worrying development of recent years is the growing right-wing sympathies among the young generation.

It is therefore essential that the pro-European Polish authorities and opinion-making agencies on all levels of social organisation such as local authorities, education and the media all coordinate their efforts to offer some interesting perspective to the youth. EU programmes promoting European liberal values and addressing youth may be welcome if they are connected with concrete opportunities. It is also worth noting that while the young men tend to vote nationalist right, young women are much more liberal in their political preferences and choice of values. They should be supported, and their self-image and confidence should be strengthened.

Portugal: Something Old, Something New and Everything Blue

Alice Cunha

In over 40 years under democracy, the Portuguese party system has been stable at the national level of parliamentary representation and government alternation as well as at the European level in the elections for the European Parliament (EP). The political parties also have a relatively linear, pro-European integration behaviour with only a few circumscribed exceptions, namely, the Communist Party's anti-European stance. This was before and shortly after Portugal's accession to the European Union (EU) and the Christian Democrats' vote against the Maastricht Treaty.

In May 2019 EP elections, 17 parties and coalitions competed, including three small, recently created parties: Alliance, Liberal Initiative and Chega (Enough which is a part of the coalition Basta!). The first two are pro-European while the latter has no clear guidelines on European affairs but instead has a populist discourse that targets mainly the political elite and immigrants.

Contrary to the situation in several member states, the populist, protest or anti-EU parties in Portugal have no media or electoral expression.

A. Cunha (✉)
Portuguese Institute of International Relations (IPRI), New University of Lisbon, Lisboa, Portugal
e-mail: alice.cunha@fcsh.unl.pt

© The Author(s) 2021
M. Kaeding et al. (eds.), *Euroscepticism and the Future of Europe*,
https://doi.org/10.1007/978-3-030-41272-2_29

However, the number of small parties have increased significantly over the past decade. Of the existing 25 parties that are officially registered, more than half have appeared in the last decade since 2015. Indeed, little is known about their positioning towards European integration and Portugal's place within the EU or any particular concrete measures. This recent creation of new parties could be interpreted as a sign of the resurgence of national civic and political participation. If we go back in Portuguese electoral history, we do find several small parties competing in various elections, both national and European, with some even succeeding in electing representatives for both the national parliament and the EP.

Moreover, in the May 2019 elections, the six parties that currently have parliamentary representation obtained more than 80 per cent of the votes, even if these votes only represent less than one third of the total number of Portuguese voters. This brings us to an old entrenched problem that political parties should be much more concerned than they actually are: abstention. Since 1976, voter turnout in legislative and in European elections has been significantly decreasing with a record abstention rate of 45.5 per cent and 69.27 per cent respectively established in the 2019 polls. Surprisingly, the Portuguese have been among the most confident in relation to the European project.

What is also odd is the fact that despite the period of crisis and economic stagnation that has witnessed three EP elections (2009, 2014, 2019), the national political system, unlike in many member states, remains resistant to change and to populist Eurosceptic parties. Strictly speaking, the vast majority of the electorate who cast their vote favour the older, more traditional, pro-European parties. Except for the new green non-Eurosceptic People-Animals-Nature (PAN) party that is the "star" party in harmony with the "green wave" that surged in the EP elections.

On the left side of the political spectrum, the Communist Party, the Left Bloc (Bloco de Esquerda) and most recently LIVRE (FREE) have a less enthusiastic approach to the state of affairs in the EU, but they are all in favour of the country's EU membership and have in no way managed to influence the government's EU policy. Despite the informal parliamentary coalition, the famous *Geringonça* or "improvised solution" that the Socialists maintained with the Communist Party and the Left Bloc over the last four years, the EU policy still remains outside the agreement.

After the last EP elections, Portugal has remained one of the few European states with no far-right party that has been elected for parliament or office. However, the Basta! coalition, despite having failed to elect its MEP, achieved a considerable result of 1.49 per cent, equivalent to almost 50,000 votes, especially given the fact that it was legalized only a few months before the election. In addition, the main party that formed the coalition (Chega—in English, Enough meaning "no more") was able to obtain significant funding for a small party and achieved a balanced consensus across the country, unlike the National Renovator Party (PNR), the oldest genuinely far-right party in Portugal which attracts votes only in the capital and has meagre electoral results (below 0.5 per cent). At that point it was correct to say that the far right and populist parties were a non-issue in Portugal.

But then something new happened. In the October legislative elections, the populist party Chega, which the media and several contenders consider to be far right despite its concerns about anti-Semitism, won 1.3 per cent of the votes (66,442 votes) and managed to elect one member of parliament (MP), the first-ever truly populist MP elected to the national parliament. Even so, one can argue that the Portuguese continue to be moderate and pro-European. The promises of quick solution to old problems combined with the growing media exposure of the party's leader, André Ventura, such as his TV football commentator supporting Benfica, Portugal's biggest football club, eventually led to his election.

Ventura is one out of 230 MPs, and neither his populist discourse nor the radical left parties with their less mainstream passionate commitment towards European integration and Portugal's place in it—which combined represent 16.94 per cent of the total vote—are expected to make a significant contribution (if any, in some cases) to EU affairs, which traditionally remain the government's prerogative. Nonetheless, the two most influential parties, the Socialists and Social Democrats—who have alternated in office and represent 64.1 per cent of the voters—should be aware and pay more attention to their constituents, particularly those who do not feel represented and, as a result, might seek a more radical representative, for instance, against the "dictatorship of Brussels" resulting in the loss of identity and sovereignty. There is still a long way to go in this respect because political parties and politicians have failed throughout the years to embed the idea that the EU is important. Is this for purely domestic and electoral purposes?

An anonymous citizen recently commented that if we were to paint in blue every part of Portugal that has benefitted, directly or indirectly, from

EU membership and EU funding, everything would be blue. So let's paint everything in blue! Let's start the first-ever serious debate on what it means in concrete terms to be European and to live in the EU, not at the level of the elites but at the level of the people, to prevent Euroscepticism from becoming established in Portugal in the near future.

Romania: Euroscepticism—Contamination of the Mainstream Parties, Limited Support Among the Citizens

Bianca Toma and Alexandru Damian

ROMANIAN EUROSCEPTICISM LOSES ELECTIONS BUT DETERIORATES THE TRUST IN THE EU

Romanians remain among the most optimistic pro-Europeans, but trust in the European Union (EU) continued to decrease in the first half of 2018. Mainstream and high-level political leaders, supported by parts of the media, are responsible for the deepening of the Romanian citizens' distrust in the EU and not only because the EU has been used as a scapegoat by the governing coalition. Forecasts for the next elections (presidential in November 2019 and local and parliamentary ones in 2020) show that citizens will, however, provide broad support to pro-European political forces and sanction populist parties, partially due to their anti-EU rhetoric but mainly due to their failure of fulfilling their electoral promises.

B. Toma • A. Damian (✉)
Romanian Centre for European Policies, Bucharest, Romania
e-mail: bianca.toma@crpe.ro; alexandru.damian@crpe.ro

Romanian Eurosceptics: Politicians Saving Themselves from Convictions

Anti-Europeanism of circumstances and defending personal and group interests is the form of Euroscepticism recently embraced by the Romanian politicians. Unlike Hungary and Poland, where political beliefs produce anti-European rhetoric, the Romanian parties have not, until recently, had broad anti-European and Eurosceptic messages. The rhetoric has changed and has been dangerously "mainstreamed" by the leaders of the ruling coalition that came to power in 2016.

The change comes amid a long campaign of the Romanian politicians in power against justice and anti-corruption investigations that have triggered the largest protests in the society since the fall of communism in 1989. Subject of numerous corruption investigations, the leading Romanian politicians supported attempts to modify and alter criminal legislation with the ultimate goal of undermining anti-corruption. These changes have significantly affected the independence of the judiciary and blocked important files of the prosecutors.

Arrogant Criticism on Brussels

These legislative amendments have been challenged by an important part of the population, opposition parties as well as the European Commission and political leaders in Brussels. Romanian politicians have responded by augmenting their anti-European messages and aggressively criticizing Brussels. Although it did not generate clear gains in the elections, this rhetoric has brought mistrust among citizens towards the EU's intentions and authority, as it seemed Brussels failed to stop the assault on justice.

An anti-European message was promoted by top politicians including the former Prime Minister of Romania, Viorica Dăncilă: "I am not here in order to give you explanations. I request to tell us who wrote the MCV reports on Romania". This was stated at the discourse at the European Parliament in October 2018.

However, Romania's most influential politician, the former president of the Social Democrats, Liviu Dragnea, is now serving 3.6 years in jail, who set the tone for an aggressive anti-EU rhetoric. Right before the 2019 European elections, Dragnea compared the Union with the "colonial powers that conquer territories for using their national resources" and was asking himself "what if they are coming after us, will we fight or accept this?"

European Elections of 2019: Heavy Losses for the Ruling Coalition

The Romanian ruling coalition suffered heavy losses in the latest round of European elections, and after two years of large pro-European and pro-rule of law protests, the elections were marked by an unprecedented high turnout (51 per cent, compared to 33 per cent in 2014) and clear gains for the pro-European parties. The ruling Social Democrats came second, with 22 per cent, tying with the newly established Alliance 2020 and clearly surpassed by the National Liberal Party. Their junior partners, ALDE Romania, did not even manage to pass the 5 per cent threshold.

This is a clear shift from the previous national elections of 2016, where the Social Democrats managed to secure over 45 per cent of the votes. On the one hand, the voters sanctioned the populist-nationalist slippage of the ruling coalition, but, on the other hand, it was a stark refusal to allow them from capturing the institutions and public resources in order to gain personal benefits. It was the latter, the attempt to capture the state powers to party politics, that the voters largely rejected.

The Social Democrats attempted to follow the footsteps of neighbouring Hungarian Fidesz party during the elections by embarking on a populist platform and using Eurosceptic views at times. They also used Brussels and other foreign actors (NGOs, multinational corporations and foreign investors) as scapegoats for not being able to deliver their 2016 promises. This type of message contrasted with what the Alliance 2020 and National Liberal Party put forward, basing their campaign on pro-European messages.

The rejection of the platform used by the Social Democrats during the elections does not mean that the dangers of Euroscepticism and populism are to be neglected in Romania. The voters have, until now, largely dismissed that using political power for personal gains was possible. The presidential elections of November 2019 witnessed a clear defeat for the candidate of the Social Democrats against the incumbent president, Klaus Iohannis. The standoff in the second round of presidential elections was won by a high margin, 66 per cent of Romanians casting their vote for Klaus Iohannis.

However, the provocative and anti-EU rhetoric constantly used in Romania took its toll. The two consecutive rounds of national elections to come in Romania in 2020, meaning parliamentary and local elections, will reshuffle the political landscape and will determine if the pro-European opposition parties will manage to maintain their current high levels of support.

Losing Citizens' Trust in the EU

The anti-European messages were not successful in these elections, but that does not mean that they did not undermine the EU's authority, capacity and image along with the Romanian public. Romanians had a higher than average scores for their trust in the EU with (52 per cent compared to 44 per cent in the EU28) according to the latest Eurobarometer (August 2019) but scored second, after the United Kingdom, when asking if they were considering EU membership a bad thing.

Support for EU membership in Romania loses 10 points (49 per cent) in 2018 with the negative view increasing by 7 points to 21 per cent, which is an unprecedented drop in support over the last ten years, the latest Eurobarometer noted coming from a level of 71 per cent recorded in the country in 2007. According to the same survey, the largest proportions of negative views on EU membership have been registered in the United Kingdom (22 per cent), Romania (21 per cent), Greece (20 per cent) and Italy (18 per cent).

What Can Be Done? Some Recommendations

Addressing Euroscepticism requires different tools that the executive branch in Brussels should have had: political and non-technocratic strategic communication with member states targeting citizens and not just the governments, while efficiently weaponizing the EU budget and EU financial and supervising mechanisms, including links of the rule of law with EU funds. The Bucharest and the post-2020 government should address this challenge by providing the framework for mitigating Eurosceptic movements, either by using better communication strategies or by enhancing support for pro-EU civic organizations and groups.

This has to be doubled by delivering good governance mechanisms and efficiently preventing any impulses, either within the government or especially populist parties, to undermine European messages and values.

Serbia: Our Greatest Fear—An Empty Country, Pawn in the Hands of Great Powers on the "Periphery of the Periphery"

Marko Savković

Serbia's fate is inseparably tied to the region of the Western Balkans. Unless key political actors make a bold and decisive step into the twenty-first century, they will remain a passive object in the hands of others, recognized today as "the third actors or countries". This will not be achieved by embracing Euroscepticism because for the Western Balkans, the European Union's (EU) greatest value is and remains one of a "peace project" that enabled reconciliation and economic development on an unprecedented scale.

Origins and manifestations of Euroscepticism in Serbia's society are manifold. One stems from the very nature of the relationship between the "center" (the EU) and the "periphery" (candidate countries). While the "center" provides concepts to emulate, the periphery acts not as a contributor but a passive receiver, with citizens either working in outsourced businesses or looking to immigrate to the "center". If projections are correct, Serbia is on the trajectory to lose one out of seven million of

---

M. Savković (✉)
Belgrade Fund for Political Excellence, Belgrade, Serbia
e-mail: msavkovic@bfpe.org

© The Author(s) 2021
M. Kaeding et al. (eds.), *Euroscepticism and the Future of Europe*,
https://doi.org/10.1007/978-3-030-41272-2_31

its inhabitants by 2050. Labour markets of the European Union and in particular Germany act like a magnet. It is no exaggeration to say that the demographic crisis in which Serbia lost 20 per cent of its population from 1989 to 2019 has emptied or is emptying entire villages and towns. Ivan Krastev has warned against this "imperative of imitation" which creates "discontents", first in Central Europe and now in the Balkans. It comes down to, what are we getting in return?

The response to the conflict in former Yugoslavia was meant to be "the hour of Europe", as Jacques Poos infamously exclaimed. It wasn't so until the United States stepped in and created in 1995 and 1999 the "Pax Americana". However, by the late 2000s, Brussels provided membership perspective. Because of the tragic experience of the 1990s, the think tank and research community has long taken for granted that the Balkans will continue to be the focus of such great powers. Today this seems rather an exception then the rule. In the aftermath of global recession and migration crisis, a new generation of politicians has taken stage, one that does not feel any kind of moral obligation and advocates a model different from liberal democracy. The impression is that the region is "left to its own devices", while positions of third actors and countries (Russia, China and to a certain degree Turkey) have become strengthened. Now, as North Macedonia—a country that has even changed its name for the sake of European perspective—and Albania were not given the green light to begin membership negotiations, this will inevitably be understood in the wider populace as the hypocrisy of "the West" and further mainstream Euroscepticism in Serbia's and other Western Balkans' societies.

The latest source of Euroscepticism is the growing rift between ideals of democracy and reality on the ground, which Srdja Pavlović was first to name "stabilocracy", referring to political developments in Montenegro. The EU key Member States have in effect traded off strict adherence to rule of law for the sake of maintaining control over: routes (used for first migrants and then illicit goods) and any potential escalation over bilateral issues. With the latest round of its "progress reports" that were critical and on point, the European Commission has managed to gain back some credibility; brought into question again with the indecision and call for revaluating the entire enlargement policy that came from France.

What furthers Euroscepticism is that there seems to be no agreement on how to proceed. On the one hand, in the aftermath of the accession of

Romania and Bulgaria, strict, merit-based approach has been developed by the European Commission (EC). This must be maintained; Croatia's recent experience shows that just before accession, the "positive pressure" of the EU is most effective. For progress to be achieved in negotiation chapters deemed as crucial—23 and 24—think tanks have proposed the methodology of the "Priebe Report", first tried in Macedonia. The problem remains with the way enlargement policy is governed, with more than 70 opportunities for individual members to stop the whole process in its tracks. Furthermore, the focus has long ago been shifted from the closing of negotiations, or individual chapters to then opening them, with no end in sight. Citizens of EU Member States being against further enlargement, and priorities of Member States diverging, capitals are keen to use this as leverage.

In Serbia, another dilemma has emerged. What should come first? The solution of the "Kosovo issue", or meeting conditions for membership? As of recently, legitimacy of ruling regime is being questioned with calls for boycotting the next elections, scheduled for Spring 2020. Meanwhile, the EU as a mediator in both conflicts is constantly being negatively portrayed, as the process implies and results in concessions for all sides. The answer for the outside observers must be that processes are important, and one must not be neglected at the expense of the other; and that the EU's role in this region and Serbia in particular remains indispensable.

Despite those who wish for status quo, in international relations it amounts only to regression or setback. Positive resolution of the political crisis in Bosnia and Herzegovina as well as the stalemate in the Belgrade-Pristina relations is in Serbia's immediate interest. Solutions must not be imposed externally; they must be "locally owned" and well thought out, and comprehensive, and their creators must bear in mind the sensitivity of the institutional arrangements that ended the wars in former Yugoslavia. They must also be legitimate and bring consensus for those who have been affected and must be obtained first. Equally important are the previous steps: in what format solutions will be sought and to stop with practices that undermine confidence. Once an agreement is reached, its implementation needs to be monitored; a major drawback of the existing ones is that the EU, in its "constructive ambiguity", did not envisage mechanisms for appeal and protection of rights, except for the political assessment by the Commission and the Council. Political actors in the region cannot do this alone and are in constant need of positive encouragement.

What Can Be Done? Some Recommendations

To conclude, a more comprehensive plan for the region is needed, but not as a substitute for full membership. It should follow the logic of the Berlin Process but be more ambitious. Whether this is a "mini Schengen", "common market" or something else experts will have their say. EU's role must remain prominent, if not leading. It should encourage key "axis" to overcome their differences. A truly regional perspective is at the same time pro-European. Overall, we become relevant only if we act together, Serbia and its neighbours.

Slovakia: Euroscepticism as a Changing Notion in Electoral Campaigns

Oľga Gyárfášová and Lucia Mokrá

EUROSCEPTICISM IN THE SLOVAK POLITICAL AGENDA

For many years Eurosceptic parties were an unknown phenomenon in Slovakia. During the pre-accession period, the European Union's (EU) integration was taken across the political spectrum as a valence issue—generally accepted as a good thing. After 2004, the broad consensus on the strategic importance of EU membership turned into a comfortable but passive consensus with respect to the European agenda and to Slovakia's performance in the EU. At least until 2011 when the Greek bail out and Slovakia's support for the European Financial Stability Facility came up in the agenda. The coalition partner liberal party Freedom and Solidarity (SaS) refused to support it (and the vote broke the centre-right government). SaS argued that the EU rejected the principle of the market economy and criticized the EU for being "too redistributive". The neo-liberal slogan "EU = road to socialism" developed into one the emerging faces of Euroscepticism. The Slovak nationalists stood for the other face and

---

O. Gyárfášová • L. Mokrá (✉)
Faculty of Social and Economic Sciences, Institute of European Studies and International Relations, Comenius University in Bratislava, Bratislava, Slovakia
e-mail: olga.gyarfasova@fses.uniba.sk; lucia.mokra@fses.uniba.sk

represented the "text-book example" of the peripheral nationalism against regional and global institutions. The nationalists' arguments go further on in losing their (national) sovereignty and identity. Nevertheless, none of these two faces became politically influential.

The new chapter of Euroscepticism in Central and Eastern Europe started with the 2015 refugee crises and the EU's relocation plan. This idea has been strictly refused (Slovakia sued the Council for the refugee distribution plan and lost the case based on the inappropriate argument of the procedural mistake in adopting the decision), but the blaming game à la "EU is imposing on us something we don't want" started and critique on the EU became more and more present in populist politics.

In Slovakia political and social atmosphere full of nationalism and anti-EU rhetoric opened the window of opportunity for the far-right extreme party People's Party of Slovakia (ĽSNS), which managed in 2016 to enter for the first time the national Parliament after general election (with 14 out of 150 mandates), following its unexpected success in the 2013 regional elections. According to the categories introduced by Paul Taggart, the party could be classified as hard-euro-sceptic—it demands Slovakia's exit from the EU and NATO. The profile of the party includes also opposing the basic principles of human rights: it rejects minority rights and makes anti-Semitic and anti-migrant statements and dehumanizing proclamations about the Roma minority.

The positions of the ĽSNS vis-à-vis the pro-European parties Progressive Slovakia and Together made the political campaign before the 2019 EP polarized as never before. The campaign contains discussions on white-collar corruption, murder of journalist in February 2018, threat to democratic foundations of Slovakia and above all the preservation of check and balances, independence of judiciary and freedom of media. The good news is the new pro-EU forces won by 20.1 per cent vote (4 out 14 Slovakia's EP mandates), but the bad news is that the hard sceptics ended up as the third strongest party with 2 mandates. The MPs did not join any political family and were too radical even for the Identity and Democracy Group. Their impact on EU policies will be practically zero, but they could sell their activities to the domestic audience by public presentations mainly through social media.

In 2016, another euro-sceptic party entered the national parliament—We are a family. This party appeals to anti-immigration stances and prior to EP election campaigned with ambitions to be a close collaborator of Mr. Salvini's League and Le Pen's National Rally with the perspective of joining the respective party family. However, the party did not manage to get over the 5 per cent threshold to be elected to the EP, partially because the migration quotas and connected agenda was not so much present as in the 2016 parliament elections.

In Slovakia so far, there is no relevant political party that would promote left-wing Euroscepticism.

The recent governmental coalition led by Smer-Social Democracy stands for pro-EU policy in all areas; in the last months it was also against the common position of V4 countries, such as the rule of law or EU-Russia relations. Also the coalition partner Slovak National Party in praxis pragmatically prefers pro-EU policy, however it from time to time comes with EU-critical statements, in praxis pragmatically prefers pro-EU policy. Though when it comes to EU the language of politicians is almost exclusively concentrated on economic and social benefits guaranteed by the EU membership, referring especially to free movement of people and funding from the EU budget. The narrative about shared values, stronger community and common policies is missing. The discussion on EU values is present in Slovakia obviously due to proceedings against neighbouring Poland because of the rule of law in violation. The Prime Minister strictly declared the recognition of the rule of law by Slovakia, and Slovak MEPs also voted for the initiating procedure against Poland and later against Hungary before the Court of Justice of the EU.

What Can Be Done? Some Recommendations

At the political parties' level: all pro-EU mainstream parties should be clear in forming a *cordon sanitaire* around the hard-Eurosceptic parties. The government should be unambiguous and show that anti-EU policy has zero coalition potential, instead of what is seen as an ad hoc instrumental voting coalition between mainstream parties and extremists.

At the public level in spite of the high public support for the country's EU membership, it is still necessary to make sure that the awareness of these benefits is not taken for granted. Different benefits of integration as peace in Europe, free movement and better environmental regulations have to be present in public discourse—including media, schools, newspapers and broadcasting. Especially the younger audiences need to be constantly reminded of what is at stake and what will be lost should the integration project fail or be reversed. The evidence-based discussions, storytelling, examples of previous and current times comparison, expert's presentations and fight against hoaxes and non-verifiable sources of information should be always present in the EU topics by all the actors.

Slovenia: Extremes Are Attractive Only to the Media

Maja Bučar and Boštjan Udovič

Just as in any other European Union (EU) Member State, Slovenia could not escape a wave of populism and Euroscepticism during the last years. Yet, it seems the ultra-left or ultra-right position to the EU was more popular in the media than with the citizens, especially if one looks at the election results in the EU Parliament in 2019. It is true that the turn-out was not very high, but interestingly enough, the Slovenian citizens recognised the benefits of membership in the EU (76 per cent of them say Slovenia was positively affected by membership in the recent Eurobarometer totally 91.5 per cent), and more than half believe that their voice counts (55 per cent), albeit only 29.8 per cent turn out to vote in the 2019 EP Parliament elections. Still, this was a higher turn-out than in previous elections for the EP, suggesting that the gradual importance of the Parliament is being recognised. Those who did attend did not give their vote to the parties most critical of the EU.

Let's look closer at what one could call Eurosceptic in the Slovenian political field. On the right, this label can be associated with the Slovenian

---

M. Bučar (✉) • B. Udovič
Centre of International Relations, Faculty of Social Sciences,
University of Ljubljana, Ljubljana, Slovenia
e-mail: Maja.Bucar@fdv.uni-lj.si; Bostjan.Udovic@fdv.uni-lj.si

© The Author(s) 2021
M. Kaeding et al. (eds.), *Euroscepticism and the Future of Europe*,
https://doi.org/10.1007/978-3-030-41272-2_33

National Party (Slovenska nacionalna stranka—SNS), led by Zmago Jelinčič Plemeniti, which is a right populist party using nationalistic and discriminative rhetoric. Their policy statements prior to the EU elections show that they are against the EU in the form envisaged by the Treaty. They are willing to accept the European countries as a league of nations with equal rights and full sovereignty as to which common policy to accept and strongly oppose the multicultural EU and argue for a strict anti-migration policy. While they did not succeed in EP elections, they do have four seats in the National Assembly and due to their rather charismatic leader, they get unproportioned amount of publicity.

Also, for the purpose of running for the EU Parliament, a new party on the far right was established, called Patriotic League (Domovinska liga— DOM), which copied its slogan from Donald Trump putting Slovenia first. Their programme was highly critical of the EU, since it opens too much room for non-EU values and traditions (especially by accepting migrants and refugees), is too centralised and therefore non-democratic. The only value they see in the EU is a common market but without the euro, which they see as a destabilising factor. To provide safety to Slovenian citizens, migration policy needs to be highly restricted and significant increase of resources should go to the police and army to assure the highest possible level of protection against any kind of migrants. The party received 1.7 per cent of all votes, which means they won no seat.

On the other side of political space, we find the Left Party (Levica), which in its policy towards the EU bears some elements of Euroscepticism. While they do not openly disagree with Slovenian membership, they argue that the EU today is in the service of corporations and capital, so deep restructuring is needed to bring it back to the people. Their election programme called for more solidarity, common social standards and democratisation of EU institutions, with a stop to market neoliberalism and nationalistic homophobic attitude towards migration.

The results of the 2019 EP elections show that Euroscepticism did not win the votes of Slovenian citizens. Even the Left Party, which prior to the elections seemed to enjoy a sufficient number of supporters to win a seat in the Parliament (with its spitzenkandidat Violeta Tomić), received only 6.43 per cent of the vote. The two far-right parties at 4.4 per cent (SNS) and 1.7 per cent (DOM) dropped even further.

The fact that the Slovenian Democratic Party (Slovenska demokratska stranka— SDS), a party with a conservative-liberal ideology, jointly with Slovenian People's Party, was the most successful at the elections (they won three seats), according to most commentators, this has less to do with their stance on EU affairs than with their popularity at home. The SDS is known for being a very disciplined body of members, who not only has a high turn-out at every election, but also loyally supports the leader of the party, Janez Janša. In the recent years, the party has moved further towards the right, with some of its members occasionally adopting populist and nationalistic rhetoric, e.g. on the immigration issue, where they oppose Merkel and support Orban's approach. On the other hand, the party does not oppose EU membership and sees Slovenia as an integral part of the Union, as long as the latter stays centre-right.

The pro-EU stance is characteristic for Social Democrats (SD; left-centre party, two seats at the European elections) and the Marjan Šarec's Party (LMŠ; left-liberal party, and also the party of the current Prime Minister's; two seats at the European elections), each succeeding in having two of their candidates elected to the EU Parliament. Looking at their political stance, some variations may be observed as to the national issues, the EU themes are treated rather similarly. Both parties are pro-EU, with SD a bit more centre-left and MSP at the centre, yet both are dedicated to Slovenian membership and convinced that this benefits Slovenia.

The failure of the Eurosceptics to attract more supporters may be explained at least by two factors: one is the fact that the overall perception of the people is that Slovenia has benefited from the EU membership. This was confirmed in the recent Eurobarometer as well as in many other more recent surveys. While the support for the membership is not as high as it was at the time of joining the EU, still has 58 per cent of those who were interviewed in Eurobarometer believe membership is a good thing for the country. Even higher was the support detected in the national survey in 2017, where 79 per cent of participants expressed their view that Slovenia should stay as a member. There are some grievances as to certain specific issues among Slovenian population, from what is commonly believed as insufficient support especially of the EU Commission. This is the case of arbitration in the decision on the border dispute between Slovenia and Croatia which lacks a strong common migration policy, but overall, the membership is accepted as the status quo.

The second reason why extreme views are not very catchy in Slovenia can be attributed to the national character. People do not like to stand out from the general opinion and mistrust those promising too much. The middle ground is considered safe and stable and that is what people prefer. While media finds it attractive to report on the ideas of Eurosceptics, these views do not get sufficient support to attract voters. What they did succeed in is to have an impact on the official migration policy, which has grown to be much more restricted over the years. Playing on the card of national security, all (except the Left) parties have agreed to changes in legislation as well as in individual actions undertaken by the government in this area. Slovenia has installed the so-called mechanical protection mechanisms (in plain language—fences and wires) on the border, which increases police and the army's presence and invests more financial resources for national security. So at least in this area, the outcry of the Eurosceptics or populists had some results, even though official data does not back such actions. In spite of increased popularity of the Balkan route, the numbers of illegal migrants are far from critical and except minor thefts and housebreaking no major security issues have been detected.

What Can Be Done? Some Recommendations

To prevent any future development of Euroscepticism, the government should pay attention to communicate the benefits of the EU membership to the Slovenian citizens. Much has already been achieved with more consistent promotion of the cohesion policy and the projects implemented in practically every Slovenian municipality. This way the EU becomes associated with something positive, close and concrete and not only as a remote bureaucracy passing complicated legislation.

Spain: The Risk of Too High Expectations on the EU's Role as a Problem Solver

Ignacio Molina

The pro-European sentiment that remains so dominant in Spain today constitutes an unlikely consensus in a country with deep political fractures both in ideology and territory. After the short period of the great constitutional agreements reached during the transition to democracy (1976–1979), the Spanish political system has adopted almost all features of majoritarian and conflict-ridden democracy regimes. This includes a style of tense relationships between the two big traditional parties (the social-democratic PSOE and the conservative PP) where there seems to be nothing to escape the confrontation. In addition to this, the long recession (2008–2013) ultimately linked to the eurozone debt crisis fuelled a rapid erosion of legitimacy of the entire polity and the emergence of a successful leftist anti-establishment party ('Podemos'). In the specific case of Catalonia, economic depression and political unrest helped to feed an increasingly virulent independence conflict, including a distressing bid for unilateral secession by the Catalan nationalists who represent almost half of the region's population which, in turn, led to a Spanish nationalist

---

I. Molina (✉)
Elcano Royal Institute, Madrid, Spain
e-mail: imolina@rielcano.org

© The Author(s) 2021
M. Kaeding et al. (eds.), *Euroscepticism and the Future of Europe*,
https://doi.org/10.1007/978-3-030-41272-2_34

backlash and the growth of a right-wing populist party ('Vox') after 2017. No one would say that political forces as disparate and confronted as those that are present in this explosive combination of left-right or centre-periphery cleavages were to share an element as central to their political programme as that of the strong support for the European Union (EU). All of them do, although it seems obvious that their respective ideas about the European utopia diverge greatly from one another. Since each party expects too much, and very differently of the integration process, there is a risk that an almost certain frustration can feed discontent, and a Eurosceptic outbreak in the medium term.

The Parties

In contrast with other European countries that show a rich panorama of Euroscepticism, since many years ago, all Spanish parties have traditionally embraced with enthusiasm the cause of the unity of the continent. The PSOE, a member of the Party of European Socialists, is currently in office and won the 2019 European Parliament elections (with 32.9 per cent of the votes) with an explicitly federalist electoral manifesto that included references to political union and a "genuine European sovereignty". The centre-right PP (which finished second, obtaining 20.2 per cent) belongs to the European People's Party and, apart from having recently adapted its logo to suit that of the EPP, officially endorsed in 2014 that "the outcome of our process of European integration should be a federal union, the United States of Europe, and not a mere union of sovereign states". For its part, 'Podemos' (with 10.1 per cent in the European elections in 2019) never adopted the Eurosceptic message that was used to be propagated widely by its Southern European partners in the United Left group, such as 'Syriza' in Greece or still today 'La France Insoumise' , since it rather preferred to blame domestic politicians and top businessmen instead of Brussels, Berlin or Frankfurt as the cause of Spaniards' problems. 'Podemos' has even stated that "advocates continuing to strengthen the political union with a new constituent reform" and "call for a profoundly pro-EU project".

In a similar Europeanist vein, the Catalan nationalist parties (which got 49 per cent among Catalan voters in the EP elections and a percentage at the national level of 7.6 per cent) started its transformation in 2012, from a dominant pragmatism to an explicit attempt to break the constitutional order, under the slogan "Catalonia, new state of Europe". The right-liberal party 'Ciudadanos' (12.2 per cent in the European elections and a member of the ALDE Party), which had been founded in Catalonia as a response to separatism and went national only in 2014, counterattacked with a "Better together" campaign that linked being part of Spain with remaining in the European Union. Even 'Vox' liked to close its campaign rallies during May 2019 election (with 6.2 per cent of votes) shouting "Long live Europe" and opted for the soft Eurosceptic ECR group in the European Parliament, instead of the harder line of far-right 'Identity and Democracy' (ID).

In short, Spanish Europeanism has always been a movement of such scope that a blue flag with twelve stars is equally waved by representatives of business, unions or the LGBT community and can be found in all Spanish political circumstances: from the King's Christmas Message to the speeches in the annual conferences of parties with sympathies for a republic—either in a march in favour of the Spanish unity or in the demonstrations organised by Catalan and Basque peripheral nationalists.

The Strong Basis of Pro-EU Attitudes

How is possible that, taking into account the majoritarian and confrontational nature of the Spanish democracy, the European policy has been so far dominated by a basic consensus in favour of the supranational integration process? The explanation relies on the strong foundations of the country's EU membership. Despite the recent accumulation of crisis, citizens and elites are still convinced that the period since Spain joined the European Community in 1986 has proved the most stable, dynamic and successful in its history. The consolidation of democracy, the social modernisation and the economic convergence with the rest of the Western world coincided with the accession in the mid-1980s and post-accession developments have been widely perceived as positive. In fact, there lies an essential part of the narrative that aims to establish that the success of the national project has finally been achieved after a long time of backwardness that resonate in the famous phrase of the philosopher Ortega y Gasset, who in 1910 sentenced that "Spain [was] itself a problem and Europe its solution".

All polls show that the indicators of confidence in the EU, after reaching a peak around 2000, then started to erode, even before the recession, but they have improved in recent years along with economic recovery. In a Eurobarometer survey conducted in 2018, when Spaniards were asked about their feelings towards Europe, 67 per cent of them declare to be attached—less than Germans, who reach a higher figure of 77 per cent but more than French (62 per cent), British (58 per cent) and Italian (52 per cent). Spaniards also believe that membership has been positive (up to 75 per cent, in a sharp contrast to the just 43 per cent of Italians, who have a positive assessment regarding benefits from being a member). Today, most citizens are in favour of deeper economic and political integration, including support for specific key policies or pillars of the EU such as the free movement of citizens, a common trade policy, an economic and monetary union, a common foreign and security policy and a common policy on migration.

But How Strong?

The consistently strong pro-European attitudes in opinion polls are matched in the political arena with parties often adopting common positions regarding EU matters, while disagreeing on most other issues. All EU Treaties (including the accession one in 1985) have been approved overwhelmingly in the Parliament. The most recent ratifications were the Treaty Establishing the European Stability Mechanism and the Treaty on Stability, Coordination and Governance; both occurred in 2012 after four years of crisis in which several deep reforms of the Spanish welfare system were adapted. Nevertheless, the Treaties passed the Congress of Deputies with around 300 votes in favour, and no more than 20 votes against. It is likely, however, that future developments of the EU integration process will not receive such incredible support, taking into account the relative robustness of the left-wing IU-Podemos coalition that is very critical of some EU decisions on economic governance and external action. The Catalan nationalist parties, even if still favourable to European integration, now show much less enthusiasm, as a consequence of the EU position following the failed unilateral declaration of independence in 2017. But it is probably the Spanish nationalist 'Vox' (which reached 15 per cent of the vote in the latest general election of November 2019 becoming the third largest party, much ahead of the pro-European 'Ciudadanos' which lost heavily until just 6.8 per cent) which may become a real Eurosceptic actor if it continues to underline with success its anti-multicultural and protectionist discourse.

If this is the case, the broad Spanish consensus regarding the main lines of Spanish EU policy may give way to a new landscape in which the more fragmented political landscape will get this rare object of consensus in Spanish politics, fractured too. The far-right rhetoric of Vox may be copied by PP in some specific policy issues, such as migration or criticism to rulings by Belgian, German or EU judges for not handing over the former Catalan regional President, Carles Puigdemont, who is sought by the Spanish Supreme Court. Conversely, Europhobic diatribes are expected among Catalan nationalists if European arrest warrant is eventually decided. A growth of Euroscepticism may also occur in the Spanish left-wing spectrum (and beyond) if another economic crisis takes and new austerity or adjustment measures have to be implemented.

What Can Be Done? Some Recommendations

In sum, the still-strong basis of Europeanism in Spain may be weaker than previously thought. The example of Italy is relevant here. It used to be a euroenthusiastic nation, similar to Spain, but its recent pattern of disenchantment with the EU is constantly growing. And, therefore, the recommendations to avoid this unlikely but not impossible future scenario affect both the EU level (it takes more mutual understanding, solidarity and effectiveness regarding economic governance, the external border or judicial cooperation) and the national level (it is healthier to overcome a naïve Europhilia and having less expectations in the EU as the solution to all domestic problems).

Sweden: Battling for Values

Gunilla Herolf

Labelling parties as Eurosceptics is not easy. The view here is that criticizing one or the other policy of integration does not merit this label but that lack of respect for EU values is equivalent to seeking to destroy the EU itself. The same view on the crucial character of values is also dominating the Swedish scene.

Currently no Swedish political party argues for leaving the EU. Two parties may, however, be labelled Eurosceptics in the sense of being overall critical of the EU. On the right-hand side are the Sweden Democrats (SD), founded in 1988, labelled by others as xenophobic, who see migration and crime as their priority issues. Its growth started only a few years ago, most likely related to the influx of migrants. The SD contends that the EU should give back power, and if not, Sweden should consider leaving. On the left-hand side, the Left Party has traditionally aimed at leaving the EU, but now seem to be on their way to changing their policy. However, the Left Party is still generally negative, arguing for power to stay with member states. They see the EU as placing market ahead of environment and not standing up for asylum and human rights.

The national elections of September 2018 became a success for the SD (17.39 percent), whereas the previous government (Social Democrats and

G. Herolf (✉)
Swedish Institute of International Affairs, Stockholm, Sweden
e-mail: gunilla@herolf.se

the Greens) lost too many votes to continue as previously. After long negotiations—based on the wish to prevent the SD from having any influence—came the January 2019 agreement. By compromising with the Centre Party and the Liberals the Social Democrats and Greens could stay in power, leaving the SD (and the Left Party) with no bargaining power in the Riksdag.

The results of the European Parliament elections of May 2019 did not come as a surprise considering that the national elections had been held fairly recently. The SD reached 15.3 percent, compared to 9.7 percent in the 2014 elections. For the other parties, the results were as follows: Left Party 6.8, Social Democrats 23.5, Green Party 11.5, Liberals 4.1, Centre Party10.8, Christian Democrats 8.6, Moderates 16.8.

A big issue is whether it is possible to cooperate with Sweden Democrats on specific issues without running the risk of being influenced by their lack of respect for certain values. The Left Party, the Social Democrats, the Green Party, the Centre Party and the Liberals are strongly against it, whereas the Christian Democrats and the Moderates seem increasingly positive. However, no cooperation has yet been initiated on national level.

SD is especially strong in southern Sweden, where they form part of the ruling coalitions in five local municipalities. In Sölvesborg, where the party gathered 29 percent, the decision was taken to forbid flying the Pride flag from the town hall during the Pride parade week. Other proposals were to stimulate and facilitate repatriation of migrants and making it more difficult for migrants to settle there. Not all initiatives can be implemented: the proposed reduction (by 25 percent) on home language education for migrant children would be contrary to Swedish law. There has been much criticism on local and national level and the Pride flag is now flying in many places in Sölvesborg.

The government's EU policies are not influenced by SD: more jobs with better conditions, an ambitious climate policy, upholding the Union's values, a common European asylum system, removal of CAP (unnecessary and benefiting already rich farmers), and budget discipline.

Also, the priorities among large parts of the population as yet seem unaffected by SD growth: In Eurobarometer (spring 2019), Swedes, like the respondents of only three other countries, saw climate change as the main concern at European level (for 21 countries immigration was priority.) The main concern on national level was the environment. Lately immigration has, however, come into focus as many political parties have announced that they don't see it as reasonable that Sweden accepts 21,000 migrants per year when neighbouring countries take 5000–8000. Brexit effects are seen as negative: Sweden loses a likeminded country that is also outside the eurozone and fears that protectionism and soft politics towards Russia may come to dominate. Views on the social dimension of the EU differ among the parties.

Sweden mainly favours intergovernmentalism, believing that some issues are better handled on the national level. The Liberal Party, however, favours closer integration (including joining the euro). Swedes are, however, on the whole, very positive to the EU: According to Eurobarometer (spring 2019) 56 percent trust the EU (no. 7), 86 percent say that they feel that their voices count (no. 1) and 83 percent say that they feel like citizens of the EU (no. 9).

What Can Be Done? Some Recommendations

Sweden should invest more in history education in schools and continually educate children in critical thinking. Young people should also be given subscriptions to good daily newspapers (to remove their entire dependence on social media).

Other political parties should challenge Eurosceptic parties on how they—outside the EU—intend to replace ERASMUS, fight international crime, terrorism etc. Today they often get away with criticizing EU solutions.

Don't let the SD "own" policy fields like migration and crime! Show them that difficult issues can't be solved in easy ways but that there are other ways to deal with them. In the same way, don't let Sölvesborg (and similar municipalities) serve as a showcase for SD policy. Instead scrutinize them to bring up the effects of SD policy.

Eurosceptics benefit by referring to the extreme waste of money through CAP (feeding rich farmers) and the EP's double location. The EU should be brave and discuss these issues.

Switzerland: A Vital Relationship in the Stranglehold of Euroscepticism

Frank Schimmelfennig

Talking about Eurosceptic parties in Switzerland requires a serious recalibration of the concept. In comparison with European Union (EU) Member States (and most European Non-Member countries), *all* Swiss parties adhere to a hard version of Euroscepticism. No Swiss party advocates a fast and full EU membership. In the Swiss context, a pro-EU party supports maintaining and expanding the Bilateral Way—the Swiss *Sonderweg* of close cooperation and deep market access through a series of intergovernmental agreements and unilateral legal adaptation—and a Eurosceptic party seeks to undo bilateralism or at the very least reduce its scope. This recalibration leaves the Swiss People's Party (SVP) as Switzerland's major Eurosceptic party.

The SVP is a prototype of the right-wing, nationalist and populist party that has thrived in much of the EU. Initially it was a small agrarian party, and combined an anti-immigration and anti-integration agenda with liberal economic positions and a populist style into a 'winning formula'. In

---

F. Schimmelfennig (✉)
Center for Comparative and International Studies (CIS), University of Zurich, Zurich, Switzerland
e-mail: frank.schimmelfennig@eup.gess.ethz.ch

© The Author(s) 2021
M. Kaeding et al. (eds.), *Euroscepticism and the Future of Europe*,
https://doi.org/10.1007/978-3-030-41272-2_36

1992, the SVP broke out of the broad pro-EU party and elite consensus and used Swiss direct democracy to mobilize an integration-sceptic majority to vote against membership in the European Economic Area. This referendum victory heralded the SVP's gradual rise to become the strongest party in the National Council (the lower house of the Swiss parliament) and to a record vote share of 29.4 percent in the 2015 elections. Even though the share decreased to 25.6 percent in the October 2019 elections, the SVP remains the largest single political force.

Moreover, the SVP's impact on Switzerland's EU policy is disproportionate to its vote share. Not only has it taken the option of EU membership off the political agenda. The SVP's capacity to campaign successfully on Swiss values such as neutrality, sovereignty and direct democracy against the alleged democratic deficits, foreign judges and power grabs of the EU constrains the institutional deepening of bilateralism. Moreover, the SVP's regular launch of popular votes against the perceived costs of integration—such as immigration or financial contributions to the EU's cohesion policy—polarizes Swiss politics and keeps EU-Swiss relations in a stranglehold.

Overall, the SVP has been more effective in constraining the future development of EU-Swiss relations than in reducing their level and scope. It mostly loses initiatives and referendums designed to withdraw Switzerland from agreements with the EU. Most recently, in September 2018, two thirds of Swiss voters accepted the 'Weapons Directive', which requires Switzerland to restrict the ownership of semi-automatic weapons in the context of Switzerland's Schengen membership even though the SVP denounced it as an anti-Swiss initiative to disarm the citizens. Even the biggest recent victory of the SVP—the 'Mass Immigration Initiative' of February 2014—fizzled when the EU refused to renegotiate the freedom of movement. The Swiss government then went for a minimalist implementation compatible with existing treaty obligations. At the end of the day, Swiss voters tend to accept concessions to the EU in order to maintain vital benefits such as Swiss access to the internal market and participation in the free-travel area. A 2018 survey shows a two-thirds majority preferring the continuation of the Bilateral Way to looser or deeper relations with the EU; 83% regard stable relations with the EU as very important.

Yet the EU pushes Switzerland to move beyond the status quo. In a major overhaul of the intergovernmental construction of the Bilateral Way, the Institutional Agreement would introduce the dynamic adaptation of market access agreements to changes in EU law. It also foresees the settlement of disputes by a joint arbitration panel and a role for the EU Court of Justice. Predictably, this institutional deepening has caused the SVP to reject the Agreement and threaten a referendum. More surprisingly, it has also drawn opposition from the left: the SP and Greens adopted the major trade unions' objection to constraints on the 'flanking measures' currently permitted to protect the Swiss market and wages. Squeezed between right and left resistance, Switzerland refrained from signing the Agreement after the negotiations had been concluded in the Autumn of 2018. Instead, the government started a consultation process and asked for 'clarification'. Annoyed by Swiss foot-dragging, the European Commission stopped recognizing the equivalence of the Swiss stock exchange at the end of June 2019. Over the summer of 2019, however, it became clear that progress was not possible before the Swiss elections and the inauguration of the new European Commission. Yet the elections have not changed the Swiss domestic baseline and the new Commission is unlikely to deviate from its predecessor. Brexit has hardened EU resistance against non-member 'cherry-picking', and uncertainty about the future EU-UK relationship prevents the EU from making further concessions to Switzerland.

What Can Be Done? Some Recommendations

The Swiss government has to stop going into hiding. It needs to sign the Institutional Agreement, start the ratification process and confront complacent expectations of better deals in the future. The EU can help this process by standing firm on the negotiated text—and by threatening to stop renewing expiring agreements that facilitate Swiss access to the EU market for goods and services. It would make clear that rejecting the Agreement will not just mean preserving a comfortable status quo but gradually losing the benefits of EU cooperation. If experience is anything to go by, chances are that a majority of voters will follow the government's EU policy if the economic stakes are higher and clearer.

The Netherlands: Playing with Fire? Dutch Political Parties Between Reluctant and Pragmatic Pro-Europeanism

Maurits J. Meijers, Lars Stevenson, and Adriaan Schout

When the Dutch prime-minister Mark Rutte, from the conservative-liberal People's Party for Freedom and Democracy (VVD), gave his Churchill lecture in Zürich early 2019, he was seen to finally opt for an unequivocal pro-European integration stance. In the European Parliament elections of May 2019, Commission Vice-President Frans Timmermans led his social democratic Labour Party (PvdA) to victory on a pro-EU platform, with the VVD and the Christian Democratic Appeal (CDA) coming in second and third place. Pro-European politics clearly took the centre stage in the Netherlands.

In March 2019, however, the Eurosceptic 'Forum for Democracy' (FvD) won the provincial elections, becoming the biggest party in the

---

M. J. Meijers • L. Stevenson
Department of Political Sciences, Radboud University,
Nijmegen, The Netherlands
e-mail: M.Meijers@fm.ru.nl; L.Stevenson@student.ru.nl

A. Schout (✉)
Clingendael, The Hague, The Netherlands
e-mail: aschout@clingendael.org

Dutch Senate. Around the same time, PM Rutte and Dutch Finance Minister Hoekstra (CDA) voiced criticism of Emmanuel Macron's ambitious plans for a common European Union (EU) budget—citing a lack of budgetary transparency as a reason. We argue that such apparent ambivalence is illustrative of the way parties and public opinion in the Netherlands have treated its relationship with the EU. There is broad support for the EU in principle and for the status quo of European integration. Yet, political parties in the Netherlands are generally wary of expanding the EU's competences, EU enlargement, as well as the 'Ever Closer Union'.

PARTIES' POSITIONS TOWARDS EUROPEAN INTEGRATION IN THE NETHERLANDS

Figure 1 shows the positions parties hold on 'European integration' (horizontal axis) as well as the percentage of the vote each party received (vertical axis). Currently five of the fifteen parties represented in the Dutch *Tweede Kamer* can be regarded as Eurosceptic, having a cumulative vote share of 28 per cent: 'Forum for Democracy' (FvD), 'Animals Party'

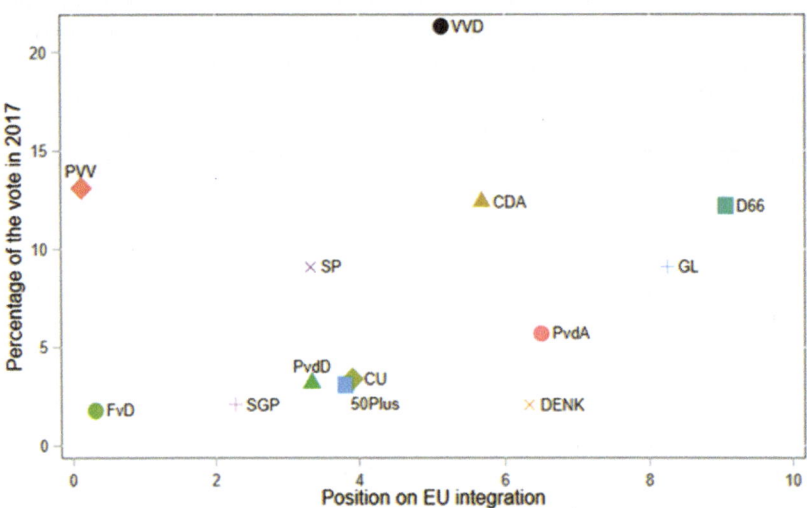

Fig. 1 Positions on European integration and vote share of Dutch political parties. (Source: Populism and Political Parties Expert Survey *(POPPA)*. www.poppa-data.eu)

(PvdD), 'Freedom Party' (PVV), 'Socialist Party' (SP), and the 'State-Reformed Party'(SGP). The PVV and the FvD take the staunchest Eurosceptic positions, with the PVV advocating a 'Nexit' and the FvD calling for a membership referendum. The PvdD, SGP and SP propose less ambitious forms of EU cooperation, with the SP arguing to leave the eurozone, the PvdD arguing for a common currency among the Northern European countries and the SGP demanding a judicial mechanism making it possible to leave the eurozone and to stay part of the EU.

Among the non-Eurosceptics, 'GreenLeft' (GL) and D66 can be regarded as outright supportive of the EU—advocating for extending EU competences in key policy areas. The position of parties such as Rutte's VVD and coalition partner CDA in Fig. 1 is a reflection of their principled support on the one hand and their reluctance to deeper integration of core state powers on the other hand. While never anti-EU as such, these parties regularly emphasize the limits to an 'Ever Closer Union'. In recent years, the VVD demanded, for instance, a system to suspend Member States from the Schengen zone. The last three governments took a tough line on net contributions to the EU, criticized economic instructions from Brussels while demanding Southern European countries strictly adhere to the Economic and Monetary Union (EMU) stability pact. Importantly, Dutch centrist parties such as the VVD, CDA and PvdA have never abandoned their support for the EU in principle.

Reluctant and Pragmatic Pro-Europeanism?

Although the rhetoric and position of the Dutch political parties and the Dutch public are widely perceived to have adopted more 'Eurocritical' tones, the levels of overall support for European integration among Dutch parties actually show very limited change over the past fifteen years. Although ruling parties have been more critical in recent years of the EU, the Dutch government, albeit not wholeheartedly, in crucial moments came out in support of EU cooperation during the financial crisis and the migrant crisis. While Dutch governments have been wary of increased pooling of sovereignty at the supranational level, they are clearly open to and pushing for strengthened cooperation among EU Member States in intergovernmental fashion. Their emphasis on rule adherence is indicative of its aim to ensure the EU's proper functioning before integrating further. For instance, despite external pressure, the Dutch have repeatedly blocked Romania's and Bulgaria's Schengen membership as well as North

Macedonia from accession talks—this does not reflect opposition to enlargement per se. Rather, the government believes the countries do not abide to the relevant accession criteria.

The same can be said of the Dutch public. Although the public has voiced stronger opposition to the EU in the previous provincial elections and only 42 per cent of Dutch having a positive image of the EU, the vote share of Eurosceptic parties has been rather stable since the 2002 national elections, as can be seen in Fig. 2, and the support for membership has always remained above 80 per cent. Branding Dutch parties and the Dutch public as Eurosceptic would miss the point. Rather, both parties and voters support integration in principle, but are wary of deeper integration. This is arguably a sign of maturation of the EU as polity and of Dutch public debate on EU affairs. It has been argued that as the authority of the EU increases, the politicization of its policies EU will too. As the EU's policy mandate increasingly covers 'core state powers', political contention over EU integration in the Netherlands is likely to intensify too. This is not necessarily a sign of increased Euroscepticism, it is merely an indication that EU policies are increasingly under public scrutiny. If we are willing to look beyond a pro-/anti-EU dichotomy, one can appreciate Dutch political parties' reluctance for deeper integration as pro-European pragmatism.

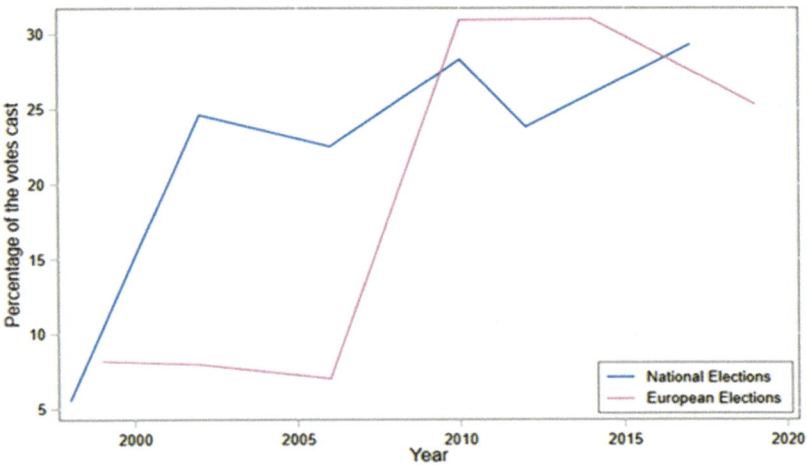

Fig. 2 Vote share of Eurosceptic parties. (Source: Parliament and Government Database (ParlGov, www.parlgov.org))

What Can Be Done? Some Recommendations

All in all, the intensity of Euroscepticism in the Netherlands has altered little in the past years, whilst the Freedom Party passed the baton to the Forum for Democracy as its principal representative. Dutch parties remain wary of federalist 'vistas', but have shown profound commitment to European cooperation as well as integration at critical times. Observers from other countries should take this to heart and should not confuse the Dutch reluctance for unwillingness to commit to Europe—despite its preferences for cooperation on an intergovernmental basis.

At the same time, Dutch mainstream parties should realize that their reluctance to unequivocally support European integration may in the long run negatively affect EU support among the Dutch public. Research has shown that political parties can 'cue' public opinion in becoming less supportive of the EU. Hence, if the parties' EU rhetoric fails to distinguish between Euroscepticism and 'pragmatic Europeanism', then this may well backfire. Dutch mainstream parties should be advised to clearly explain their 'pragmatic Europeanism' to the Dutch public and demarcate it from Euroscepticism, or risk losing support for their pragmatic EU position in the long run.

Turkey: A Vicious Cycle of Euroscepticism?

Senem Aydın-Düzgit and Özgehan Şenyuva

Relations between Turkey and the European Union (EU) are currently facing an impasse. After a long period of stagnation, accession negotiations, which began in 2005, are now *de facto* frozen. Recent public opinion polls in Europe record an all-time low popularity of Turkish membership across the European public, whereas the European political elite has long dropped the discourse on Turkish accession in favour of a "strategic partnership" with Turkey.

Against this background, it is not surprising that recent public opinion polls point to a growing degree of Euroscepticism across the Turkish public. In a rather polarized society between the government and opposition, mistrust of the EU and anti-Western attitudes remain among the rare islands of agreement between the two blocs. Public support for Turkey's membership to the EU currently floats at around 30 per cent, which was averaging around 75 per cent in the first half of the 2000s. The trust on

---

S. Aydın-Düzgit (✉)
Sabancı University, Istanbul, Turkey
e-mail: senem.aydinduzgit@sabanciuniv.edu

Ö. Şenyuva
Centre for European Studies—Middle East Technical University (CES-METU), Ankara, Turkey

the eventuality of Turkey's membership is also very low, with the majority of the public believing that regardless of what Turkey does, it will never be allowed to become an EU member.

The situation also looks bleak when we turn to Turkish political parties. Although there is not an explicitly anti-EU party in the political scene, anti-European discourse based on unfair and unjust treatment of Turkey is a dominant theme. Since its second electoral victory in 2007, the governing AKP and its leader Erdoğan have increasingly resorted to Eurosceptic discourse in the public sphere replacing the positive representations in AKP's initial years in power. The European Other is now mostly constructed as an 'unreliable and untrustworthy partner', an 'unwanted intruder in Turkish politics', an 'essentially discriminatory entity' with fixed civilizational differences with Turkey, and as an entity that is 'democratically/politically/ morally inferior to Turkey'. Rather than a radical rupture, the new AKP discourse towards Europe contains elements of continuity as well as change with previous political party articulations on Europe. The representation of Europe as morally inferior can be traced back to the 1960s, and the representation of Europe as an unwanted intruder resonates with the rise of the Sèvres syndrome since the 1970s, which entails the fear of territorial partition by European powers. However, following 2007, these representations became dominant and officially endorsed. In addition, novel representations, such as the Europeans being unreliable partners who do not follow up on their commitments, such as those stemming from the EU-Turkey refugee deal, have also been articulated in the party's discourse.

The main opposition party, CHP, seems to espouse a more pro-European discourse. This has not always been the case, as the party largely espoused a Eurosceptic stance during the short-lived era of AKP's Euro-enthusiasm. This has changed with the change in party leadership in 2010 where it countered the AKP's Eurosceptic discourse with a pro-European one, particularly in relation to issues concerning democracy. Yet, the highly limited freedom of expression in Turkey means that there are significant constraints on the extent to which this Euro-enthusiast discourse reaches the Turkish public. Furthermore, the party has to balance this pro-European discourse with the dominant anti-European sentiments also present in its own constituency.

There are multiple reasons that can account for the increase of negative sentiments that Turkish citizens harbour towards the EU. Some point at the role of the EU's reluctance to admit Turkey as a future member and the mistrust that this has bred in the Turkish context, while others underline the significance of increased Turkish self-confidence and perceived superiority over Europe in the last decade or the AKP's purposeful efforts in cultivating Eurosceptic political narratives which were found to have had a wide influence across its supporters among the Turkish public. It can be argued that the EU member states' positions and policies vis-à-vis the Syrian refugees also played a role in shaping Turkish perceptions. For many, it is the EU that is drifting away from the values over which it has claimed ownership, while Turkey hosts close to 4 million Syrians despite the economic downturn.

There are also other, more constant explanations, which are advanced as long-durée factors that underlie Euroscepticism in Turkey, such as fears over the loss of moral values, and strong attachments to national identity including concerns over the loss of national sovereignty. As for political parties, the AKP's Euroscepticism can be accounted for by both ideology and self-interest. The religious-nationalist identity which the party articulates both in discourse and practice is an essentialist and exclusivist one which rests on a substantial distancing and negative representation of Europe. This is bolstered with the rise of right-wing populism and nativism in the EU, providing ammunition to claims that the EU by essence is an Islamophobic Christian club. On the policy front, the party is particularly uncomfortable with the EU's stance on the state of Turkish democracy, which places it in a starkly opposite corner in matters relating to domestic governance.

As of today, there are roughly three groups in the EU which all advocate a different type of relationship with Turkey. One group is the absolute naysayers to Turkey within Europe, who would utilize any opportunity, including the political situation in Turkey, to justify their rejectionism. Their actions and rhetoric provide fuel to Turkish Euroscepticism, leading to a downward spiral. The second group consists of transactionalists who prefer to work with Turkey on issues of interest, such as security, energy, and migration, regardless of the political situation and the level of democracy in Turkey. The third group, albeit being in minority, continues to strive for a relationship based on rules and values.

What Can Be Done? Some Recommendations

The future of Euroscepticism in Turkey as well the course of the relationship between the two will ultimately depend on the constellation of power between these groups as well as their engagement with the domestic developments within Turkey. The divergence between Turkey and the EU cannot be overturned easily, as it requires fundamental political and social changes both in Turkey and in other European states. The EU should engage with parts of Turkish civil society which still strive for democratic governance and invest in pluralistic and constructive voices on both sides. Despite the political situation in Turkey, it should refrain from taking radical political steps such as the suspension of accession negotiations which would most likely be instrumentalized by the government to foster Euroscepticism at home. In Turkey, it is imperative that Euroscepticism is not utilized for short-term domestic political gains. Only then a defensive line may be established to prevent the relations from becoming purely transactional or being ruptured.

UK: Brexit—The Car That Keeps on Crashing

Brendan Donnelly

The result of the European referendum on British membership of the European Union in 2016 represented at one level a political triumph for the United Kingdom's Independence Party (UKIP) and its leader Nigel Farage. For twenty years his party was the only organised political body advocating British withdrawal from the EU. The autonomous influence of UKIP should not however be overstated. UKIP's success has largely derived from its capacity to influence and threaten the two major parties of the British political system.

The first major political success for UKIP was in the European Elections of 1999. Although later UKIP somewhat broadened its appeal, most of its support in 1999 came from disaffected Conservative voters. Ever since, the European policy of the Conservative Party has been influenced by the fear of losing electoral support to UKIP. Conservatives sympathetic to UKIP's desire to leave the EU have relentlessly exploited this fear in order to drive their Party in a radically Eurosceptic direction. David Cameron's pledge of an EU referendum, originally announced in 2013,

---

B. Donnelly (✉)
Federal Trust, London, UK
e-mail: brendan.donnelly@fedtrust.co.uk

was an attempt to conciliate the warring factions within his Party. It succeeded in briefly uniting the Conservatives and allowing them to win the General Election in 2015. Its consequences in the longer term were very different to Cameron's hopes and expectations.

While no enthusiast for the European Union, Cameron had come to believe as Prime Minister that there was no rational alternative to continuing British membership of the EU. His miscalculation put an end to his Premiership and assured the final triumph in his Party of uncompromising Euroscepticism. The absolute nature of this triumph was to some extent disguised by the tentative and compromising Premiership of his successor, Theresa May. Her successor, Boris Johnson, reflects in his rhetoric and announced policies the settled desire of today's Conservative Party to incorporate within its ranks all previous UKIP voters and supporters of UKIP's successor, the Brexit Party.

A number of factors contributed to the success of the pro-Brexit campaign in 2016. The Remain campaign was lacklustre and hesitant, while the Leave campaign was energetic and unscrupulous. Many voters saw the referendum as an opportunity to vote against an unpopular Conservative government. Twenty years of anti-EU propaganda by prominent newspapers created fertile ground for the simplistic and sometimes dishonest arguments of the Leave campaign. The unwillingness of the Leader of the Labour Party, Jeremy Corbyn, to campaign wholeheartedly or collaboratively with members of other political parties was a check on the effectiveness of the Remain campaign.

Since the referendum of 2016, the attitude of Jeremy Corbyn to Brexit has assumed increasing importance. He has steadfastly resisted attempts by the majority of his Party to adopt as Labour policy an unequivocal opposition to Brexit. He has found some support for this equivocal position from those within his Party concerned that the Brexit Party (formerly UKIP) might do electoral damage to the Labour Party among some of its traditional voters. While opposing a "Conservative no deal Brexit," he has made clear that his preferred option is a "Labour Brexit" that will supposedly safeguard jobs and respect the rights of workers. He persuaded the Labour Party conference in September,2019 to adopt as party policy a commitment to attempt to negotiate just such a "Labour Brexit" if the party is returned to power in a forthcoming General Election. This "Labour Brexit" would then be put to the electorate in a fresh referendum.

A small majority of those voting in 2016 were willing to embrace the unrealistic expectations that Brexit promised. The uninformed and distorted nature of the European debate in the UK had its roots not just in 2016, but in the decades that preceded it. This failure of political discourse is the responsibility of pro-EU politicians in the UK almost as much as the EU's opponents. Pro-EU politicians in the UK have been unwilling to explain to British voters that the processes of sovereignty-sharing and integration intrinsic to membership of the EU are unequivocally in the British national interest. Instead they have taken refuge behind opt-outs and rebates, behind special arrangements and unilateral declarations supposedly designed to protect the UK from a burgeoning European superstate.

After the General Election of 12th December and the Conservative victory, it now seems inevitable that the UK will leave the European Union on 31st January, 2020. The European Elections of May 2019 allowed the Brexit Party to win more seats than any other party, but the overall votes cast in the Elections for parties favourable to Brexit and those hostile to Brexit were approximately equal. This equilibrium led some to expect a similarly indecisive result in the General Election at the end of the year. Instead the Conservative Party won a substantial victory, greatly aided by the unpopularity of the main leader of the Opposition Jeremy Corbyn. With this victory, any possibility of delaying Brexit or making it subject to a referendum has been finally extinguished. The next stage of the Brexit tragicomedy now moves to the negotiations after January 2020, for which Boris Johnson claims to envisage an implausibly rapid and favourable outcome. The collision between such optimistic aspirations and the reality of negotiating as a third party with a trading superpower such as the EU will be a painful one for Johnson and his supporters. A favourite Conservative mantra during the General Election was that of "getting Brexit done." But the UK's formal exit from the EU on 31st January 2020 will be far from getting Brexit "done." To adapt a famous Churchillian phrase, 31st January 2020 will not be the end of Brexit. It will not even be the beginning of the end. It will at most be the end of the beginning.

What Can Be Done? Some Recommendations

The Remain side could certainly have won a referendum in 2020 if they avoided the mistakes of 2016, among which was the apologetic and unenthusiastic tone of the Remain campaign. There is a widespread view among commentators in the UK that enthusiasm for the EU is counterproductive in campaigning about Europe. This article closes with the firm assertion that the best way for British voters to start feeling enthusiastic for the EU is for British advocates to manifest more of that enthusiasm themselves. Bitterness and resentment are infectious emotions. However, and just as powerfully, so are enthusiasm and commitment. Pro-Europeans in the UK should show more of the latter if they want to win a future referendum.

Ukraine: The Progress of (Euro) Populism in Postmodern Age

Yuriy Yakymenko and Viktor Zamiatin

The results of the 2019 national elections in Ukraine echoed all-European and global trends. The outcome of the presidential and parliamentary elections suggest that Ukrainians have resolutely refused to support well-known politicians, parties and systemic politics in general. However, Ukraine is notable for the lack of significant public support for radical political forces.

The nationalists have no parliamentary faction since 2014, and polls consistently show the downward trend in their support. Also, despite the society's general disposition to the leftist programme elements, including strong social support, protection of the poor, free education and health care, and a ban on the land market, the leftist forces also lack the public support.

In the Ukrainian context, the Europe-wide trend of growing Euroscepticism as a protest against the Brussels bureaucracy looks like a transformation of public support for reforms aimed at joining the EU towards support for a kind of "European populism".

Y. Yakymenko • V. Zamiatin (✉)
Razumkov Centre, Kiev, Ukraine
e-mail: yakimenko@razumkov.org.ua; zamiatin@uceps.com.ua

© The Author(s) 2021
M. Kaeding et al. (eds.), *Euroscepticism and the Future of Europe*,
https://doi.org/10.1007/978-3-030-41272-2_40

The parties that have been in power since 2014 (Petro Poroshenko Bloc "Solidarity" and the People's Front) have declared the preparation for Ukraine's EU and NATO accession along with implementation of necessary reforms as the heart of the state policy. Endless criticism of the government for the growing energy prices and ensuing increase in utility tariffs, for deteriorating living standards, as well as for corruption by members of various political forces, further fuelled by the most popular TV channels, has significantly undermined the positions of these "Euro-reformists".

While being perfectly aware of the real reasons for such situation—the war with Russia and the IMF requirements—some party leaders have unreasonably promised, for example, a two-fold reduction in tariffs to their voters.

Unrealistic social commitments of politicians (manifold increase in wages, reduction of prices and tariffs, etc.) have become a turning point in public opinion, with the parties that once also declared their commitment to the European idea transforming into the main critics of the "Euro-reformist" government.

The fierce political struggle within the "pro-European" camp has resulted in the disastrous loss of positions by all parties and leaders involved, the loss of public confidence in the state institutions, and the emergence of new figures. The latter include president Zelensky and his party "Servant of the People". A year prior to elections, the party was non-existent, while Mr. Zelensky enjoyed the fame of a comedian, a TV producer and the leader of a comic group, which in its sketches gave a hard time to many politicians, "Euro-reformists" and the West and its liberal attitudes.

Zelensky and his entourage were able to construct a parallel reality in which they offered themselves as brand new leaders for the country, and "sold" it to society. This postmodern reality simply had no room for traditional parties. Mainstreaming the division into "new" and "old" politicians was a response to the untapped public demand for new politicians and the new quality of politics, which converged the agendas of different social groups.

In this situation, the true Eurosceptics also had no gains. In the current parliament, this role is played by the faction of the Opposition Bloc—For Life. It stands for Ukraine's departure from association with the EU and movement towards NATO, while insisting on political and economic rapprochement with Russia (despite the war waged by the latter). This party has no influence on the formation of the government, and the number of its supporters is not growing.

As a result, Ukraine received two types of opposition with contrasting views—the pro-European "European Solidarity" on the one hand, and the anti-European and pro-Russian Opposition Platform—For Life on the other. Both remain on the margins of political life.

The unprecedented support of Zelensky (over 73% of votes in the second round of the presidential elections) and his party "Servant of the People" (43% of votes in the parliamentary elections) by Ukrainians led to a three-quarters renewal of the parliament and the establishment of a one-party government configuration. The figure of president Zelensky, just like his party "Servant of the People", brought together people with diverse (or absent) political views and values—supporters of European integration and Eurosceptics (those who do not view the EU membership as a priority), backers of the liberal and socialist economy, as well as supporters of Ukraine's NATO membership and nonalignment.

As a presidential candidate, Zelensky did not make any specific promises other than claims to change everything and "break the system". Zelensky's electoral programme was written by his team based on voters' "wishes" collected via social media. Moreover, it is impossible to determine the "Servant of the People" ideology due to its mere absence.

The European integration (albeit in rather uncertain form) is still among the political priorities of the new government, as some of its members once worked really hard to bring Ukraine closer to the EU, and some worked in the EU-funded projects (including ex-PM Honcharuk and several ministers, resigned on March, 4, 2020). That is, the society's demand for continuation of European integration policy is at least taken into consideration.

The rhetoric of government representatives is based on persistent appeals to the will of the people, which is a traditional attribute of populism. The new president and his party seek to make the most of their monopoly power largely in defiance of the opposition, mass media, or civil society.

As a result, Ukraine's European integration lies in the hands of political forces that are more likely to respond to situational societal sentiment, which poses certain risks. Accordingly, the government's "pro-European" rhetoric can easily shift towards "Euroscepticism". Moreover, the new government already head for revision of some reforms initiated in the process of Ukraine's European integration.

What Can Be Done? Some Recommendations

In general, the Ukrainian situation complements the general picture of today's postmodern world, characterised by post-truth and multiple alternative realities. At the same time, the weakness of the state and public institutions, the war and the economic situation against the background of pan-European turbulence pose a number of very serious challenges for the entire country.

Index

A
Agenda-setting, 53
Albania, x, 1–4, 15, 80, 128
Asylum, 63, 66, 71, 110, 116, 145, 146
Austria, x, xii, xv, 5–8

B
Belgium, v–xvii, 9–12, 96
Border, v, vii, 7, 11, 37, 57, 62, 66, 78, 79, 96, 137, 138, 143
Bosnia and Herzegovina, x, 13–15, 129
Brexit, v, xi, 36, 37, 44, 70–72, 76, 95, 112, 113, 147, 151, 163–166
Bulgaria, xiv, 17–20, 44, 129, 155

C
Civil society, vi, ix, xvi, xvii, 2, 12, 39, 51, 58, 116, 162, 169
Climate change, xvi, 7, 146
Coalition, xi, xiv, xv, 5–7, 18, 21, 22, 30–32, 40, 41, 44–46, 52, 53, 56, 62, 65, 67, 73–75, 90, 93, 98, 101, 102, 111, 112, 115, 116, 119–121, 123–125, 131, 133, 142, 146, 155
Cohesion, vi, xvi, 11, 58, 60, 71, 83, 138, 150
Competences, 10, 44, 59, 64, 154, 155
Crisis, x, 17, 26, 27, 30, 39, 40, 44, 48, 51, 52, 56, 66, 74, 75, 93, 117, 120, 128, 129, 139, 141–143, 155
Criticism, 2–3, 6, 7, 10, 11, 30, 45, 49, 86, 87, 90, 94, 124, 143, 146, 154, 168
Croatia, x, xii, 21–23, 129, 137
Cyprus, xi, xii, 25–28
Czech Republic, 31

D
Debate, vi, x, xiv, xvii, 12, 15, 19, 20, 23, 26–32, 36, 42–46, 50, 66, 68, 70, 85–87, 91, 92, 122, 156, 165

172 INDEX

Democracy, v, vi, xi, xvi, 19, 20, 32, 48, 60, 71, 72, 86, 94, 98, 111, 117, 119, 128, 139, 141, 150, 160, 161
Denmark, xi, xii, xv, 35–38
Digital, 11, 39, 58

E

Elections, v, vi, ix, xi, xii, xv, 4, 6, 7, 9–12, 17, 19, 21–23, 26–28, 30, 31, 35, 36, 40, 41, 44–53, 55–57, 60–62, 66, 67, 70, 73–75, 79, 81, 82, 86, 87, 89–94, 97–99, 101–103, 106, 110, 111, 117, 119–121, 123–126, 129, 132, 133, 135–137, 140–142, 145, 146, 150, 151, 153, 156, 165, 167–169
Enlargement, xvii, 3, 4, 11, 57, 63, 71, 79, 80, 96, 103, 105, 106, 116, 117, 128, 129, 154, 156
Environment, vi, 46, 60, 61, 83, 145, 146
Estonia, xii, 39–42
EU budget, 99, 126, 133, 154
EU Council, xv, 6, 45
EU Member States, vi, vii, x, xiii, 2, 41, 46, 66, 68, 70–72, 74, 83, 91, 110, 118, 126, 128, 129, 135, 149, 155, 161
Euro, 22, 23, 26, 27, 37, 43, 49, 52, 55–57, 136, 147, 167–170
Eurobarometer, xi, 1, 9, 26, 31, 35, 40, 43, 57, 83, 91, 98, 102, 126, 135, 137, 141, 146, 147
European Economic Area (EEA), xiii, 65–68, 85–88, 111, 112, 150
European Financial Stability Facility, 131
European Free Trade Association (EFTA), xiii, 65, 67, 87, 88, 110

European Parliament (EP), v–xvii, 7, 10–12, 17, 19, 22, 28, 31, 35, 36, 41, 45, 52, 56, 57, 61, 73, 75, 82, 89, 90, 94, 95, 97–99, 117, 119, 120, 124, 132, 133, 135, 136, 140, 141, 147
European Parliament elections, xi, xii, 10, 11, 26, 28, 31, 45, 82, 140, 146, 153
European Union (EU), v, 1–5, 9, 14, 17, 21, 25, 30–32, 35–39, 43–46, 48, 51, 55, 59, 65, 69, 73, 77–81, 85, 89, 94, 97, 101–109, 115, 119, 123, 126, 127, 131, 135, 139–143, 145, 149, 154, 159, 163, 167
Euroscepticism, ix–xvii, 1–4, 8, 11, 13–15, 17, 18, 21, 23, 25, 27–30, 35, 41, 44, 45, 47–51, 53, 55–64, 69–72, 74, 77–79, 81–92, 94, 97–104, 106–108, 110, 113, 116, 119–128, 131–133, 135, 136, 138, 140, 143, 149–151, 156, 157, 159–162, 164, 167, 169
Eurozone, xii, xiii, 18, 22, 26, 32, 51, 55, 75, 81, 83, 92, 139, 147, 155
Expectations, vii, 14, 26, 36, 103, 139–143, 151, 164, 165

F

Far-right, xii, xiv, xv, 21, 22, 36, 43, 45, 47, 48, 51, 56, 57, 62, 99, 106, 120, 121, 132, 136, 141, 143
Finland, xiv, 43–46
Foreign policy, 79, 89, 92, 101, 102
France, xi, xii, 15, 47–50, 76, 80, 105, 128
Future of Europe, vii, 15, 44, 53, 58

G

Germany, xiv, 35, 37, 51–53, 76, 117, 128
Government, ix, x, xiv–xvii, 3, 6, 7, 11, 17–23, 25, 27, 28, 30–33, 37, 38, 40, 41, 44–46, 50, 52, 53, 56–59, 61–67, 70, 71, 73–76, 83, 87, 93–96, 99, 103, 107, 111, 112, 118–121, 126, 131, 138, 145, 146, 150, 151, 155, 156, 159, 162, 164, 168, 169
Greece, xi, xiv, 44, 52, 55–58, 126, 140
Green, 73, 75, 76, 120, 128

H

Hungary, xii, xiv, xv, 6, 32, 59–64, 83, 124, 133

I

Iceland, x, xiii, 65–68
Identity, 32, 48, 58, 75, 92, 95, 106, 116, 121, 132, 161
Immigration, xi, xv, xvi, 6, 11, 19, 36, 41–43, 45, 46, 52, 57, 86, 108, 137, 146, 150
Integration, ix, x, xiii–xvii, 2–4, 6–12, 14, 15, 18, 33, 38, 40–42, 46, 47, 49–53, 57, 58, 60, 65, 67, 71, 77–79, 82, 83, 85–87, 90, 92, 96, 98, 101–103, 105–108, 115–117, 119–121, 131, 133, 140–142, 145, 147, 150, 153–157, 165, 169
Intergovernmentalism, xii, 82, 83, 147
Ireland, 35, 69–72, 91
Italy, 62, 73–76, 126, 143

K

Kosovo, 77–80

L

Latvia, xii, 81–84
Left-wing, xii, xv, 21, 55, 57, 59, 70, 79, 102, 115, 117, 133, 142
Liechtenstein, x, xiii, 85–88
Lithuania, xii, xiii, 89–92
Luxembourg, 93–96

M

Maastricht Treaty, x, 47, 119
Malta, xii, 97–100
Media, vi, ix, x, 2, 12, 29, 40, 50–52, 60, 62, 83, 89, 91, 94, 99, 103, 118, 119, 121, 123, 132, 133, 135–138, 147, 169
Migration, v, xi, xv, 6, 7, 18, 19, 32, 40, 44, 48, 53, 57, 58, 60, 61, 71, 74–76, 83, 98, 99, 103, 128, 133, 136–138, 142, 143, 145, 147, 161
Montenegro, x, 78, 101–104

N

Nationalism, vi, vii, xv, 13, 18, 59–64, 70, 74, 106, 110, 115, 116, 132
The Netherlands, 44, 66, 76, 153–157
North Atlantic Treaty Organization (NATO), 1, 2, 39, 91, 103, 106–108, 132, 168, 169
North Macedonia, x, 15, 17, 57, 63, 80, 105–108, 128, 155–156
Norway, x, xiv, 68, 109–113

O

Opt-out, 36, 37, 86, 165

P

Periphery, 69, 71, 98, 109, 127–130
Poland, xi, xii, 32, 83, 115–118, 124, 133

Policies, vi, vii, x, xiv–xvi, 6, 10, 11, 18, 19, 22, 27, 31–32, 36, 37, 39, 42–46, 48–53, 55, 57–59, 61–64, 66, 67, 69, 70, 76, 80, 83–85, 87, 89–92, 94, 95, 98, 99, 101–103, 105–108, 110, 120, 128, 129, 132, 133, 136–138, 141–143, 145–147, 150, 151, 155, 156, 161, 163, 164, 168, 169

Political parties, ix, xii, xiii, xv, 2, 4, 10–13, 18, 21, 22, 26, 29–31, 39, 40, 43, 44, 46, 51, 53, 65–67, 70, 77–79, 81, 82, 85, 87, 88, 90–92, 95, 101–103, 106, 107, 111, 119–121, 133, 145–147, 153–157, 160, 161, 164

Populism, vii, xiii, 17–20, 36, 57, 70, 77, 106, 125, 135, 161, 167–170

Portugal, 119–122

Public opinion, xi, 2, 5, 41, 57, 90, 106, 154, 157, 159, 168

R

Radical, xv, 6, 9, 10, 30, 40, 41, 45, 48, 49, 56, 57, 71, 115, 121, 132, 160, 162, 167

Referendum, x, xii, 5, 23, 37, 47, 48, 57, 75, 82, 93, 94, 98, 106, 109, 111, 113, 150, 151, 155, 163–166

Romania, 44, 123–126, 129, 155

Rule of law, vi, 3, 8, 60, 63, 72, 107, 117, 126, 128, 133

Russia, 19, 41, 60, 83, 91, 107, 128, 147, 168

S

Schengen, xiii, 18, 44, 49, 62, 65–68, 92, 110, 150, 155

Serbia, x, 79, 127–130

Slovakia, xii, 131–133

Slovenia, 135–138

Sovereignty, xvi, 7, 20, 36, 37, 40, 41, 48, 51, 66, 87, 90, 111, 112, 116, 121, 132, 136, 150, 155, 161

Spain, xv, 91, 139–143

Sweden, x, xiv, 37, 145–147

Switzerland, x, xiii, xvi, 2, 85, 87, 113, 149–151

T

Trust, vi, vii, xvii, 2, 3, 9, 19, 25, 26, 31, 40, 76, 91, 92, 112, 123, 126, 147, 159

Turkey, x, xvii, 11, 26, 60, 62, 128, 159–162

U

Ukraine, xi, 60, 63, 91, 167–170

United Kingdom (UK), v, x, 31, 37, 71, 72, 91, 95, 100, 109, 110, 163–166

V

Von der Leyen, Ursula, 62, 63, 75

W

Western Balkans (WB), xiii, xvii, 3, 57, 63, 79, 80, 103, 105, 106, 127, 128

CPI Antony Rowe
Eastbourne, UK
September 10, 2020